G000077211

Dropsh

E-Commerce Business Model 2020

A step-by-step guide for beginners on How to Start a Dropshipping E-Commerce Business and Make Money Online

Best Financial Freedom Books & Audiobooks

Robert Kasey

Table of Contents

Introduction

To make a living in the past, you would have to get a job and work all the days of your life. If you don't want to go the job route, you would need to start your own business. Most people who lived in the past just got jobs because it was the most natural option for them. Most of the jobs were very tedious and required a lot of physical strength. No wonder people still detest going to work even up till this day even though most of the jobs we do today don't require a lot of physical strength.

For those who wanted to start a business in those days, they needed a lot of money. There were just a lot of things to be paid for. You would need money to acquire a business space, do the necessary registrations, obtain all the licenses, pay staff remuneration and bear huge risks. All these made starting a business in those days very hard and an option that was only available to a few.

I am not trying to imply that starting a business today is easy, but it is relatively easier compared to what was obtainable in the past. In those days, there were not a lot of tools that would make your business grow fast and flourish. However, we now have so many tools at our disposal that we could deploy and grow our business. We have a lot of business options or models available that a smart entrepreneur can exploit, unlike in those days that the possibilities were limited.

Today, thanks to the internet, starting and running a business is not seen as something reserved for a few. The internet has introduced a paradigm shift in the way we do most things. From the way we eat to the way we interact with each other, the internet has changed it all. An aspect of our existence in which the internet has played a critical, decisive role is in the way we do business.

There has never been a time in the history of humankind that starting and running a profitable business has been as easy as it is today. This ease of doing business that the internet has brought made it possible for different types of online and offline businesses to spring up. Today, we have blogging as a form of business which is putting a lot of money in the pockets of smart entrepreneurs. We also have affiliate marketing, eCommerce, and a host of other types of online businesses.

The interesting fact is that starting any of these mentioned types of online businesses does not cost so much money. In most cases, you need a computer, internet connectivity, and a little money to pay for subscriptions. Once you have sorted out these things, then you are already in business. This is why I mentioned earlier that there has never been a time in history that doing business was easier than now. No wonder we now have so many young people who make millions just from the comfort of their bedroom.

One type of online business model that has gained grounds in the past few years and will continue to grow in popularity is eCommerce. People used to walk down to the store down the road to get supplies, but we have become so lazy. Technology has continued to make us desire the easy way out. So, more and more people are now resorting to buying the things they need online.

Large scale internet penetration has made e-commerce become a vast industry. And in the coming years, as more and more people continue to adopt easier ways of shopping, e-commerce will continue to grow. This is why e-commerce is one of the best online businesses that a smart entrepreneur should start today.

The word e-commerce is derived from two words, electronic and commerce. It simply means commerce that is performed on electronic devices or over the internet. Ecommerce is a wide field – there are different types. We have retail arbitrage, white labeling, online wholesaling and retailing, etc. which are all different forms of e-commerce.

In this definitive guide, we shall be focusing our attention on one type of e-commerce, known as dropshipping. The word dropshipping seem to be on the lips of everyone recently, but only a few people truly understand what it really means. Dropshipping is not a new concept or idea – you might have dropshipped in the past without knowing it. Dropshipping is the easiest way to get into the e-commerce space. It requires a minimal investment of capital and effort. In fact, as a dropshipper, you are basically a middleman who sells other people's products without even seeing or touching the products.

So, what is dropshipping, how does one go into it, what are the best tips for success as a dropshipper? What are the best dropshipping platforms for anyone? How can someone create their own dropshipping platform? All these and more are what we shall be discussing in this guide. Without further ado, let's get started.

Chapter One:
What is dropshipping?

Dropshipping is an online business that involves connecting a potential buyer of a product with a seller or supplier. What happens is that you as the dropshipper is only but a middleman between a supplier and buyer of a product.

It is a type of retail system where you don't have to keep inventory – your job is to find someone who wants to buy a product and then connect them with a supplier. If a buyer indicates interest that they want to buy a product, you will go scouting for a supplier that has the product. Next, you take money from the buyer, pay some of the money to the supplier, and give the supplier the address of the buyer. The supplier then packages the product and ships to the buyer, and the transaction becomes complete.

In order to reach a wider audience of buyers, you will need to create an online store. Once created, you will need to populate your online store with products that the buyer needs. You will write clear product descriptions for each product so that the buyer knows exactly what they are about to buy.

Ideally, what you are creating is a typical online store. However, unlike conventional online stores where the owners need to have an offline inventory; as a dropshipper, you are not keeping any inventory. The reason is simple - you are not selling your own products; you are instead selling the products of other people.

After you have created your online store, you market it or send traffic to it so that buyers who want the products you have listed could contact you and place an order. Once an order has been placed, you take the money paid by the buyer and then head over to the supplier. You pay part of the money to the supplier so that they ship the good or product to the buyer.

It is just like your typical buying and selling or what is called retail arbitrage. However, in everyday buying and selling, a seller would buy from a cheaper source, keep the product in their store or inventory house, and look for buyers. When a buyer comes around, the seller hands over the desired product to the buyer. Dropshipping is a bit similar; however, you are not keeping an inventory of any kind.

You don't even get to see the good or products you are selling. You only list them on your online platform, and when you are contacted or when an order is placed, the supplier sends the product directly to the buyer.

How do you make a profit as a dropshipper? Your profit is the difference between the price for which you listed the product and the actual price that the supplier has set for the product. For instance, if a headset sells for $100, you could set the price at $150. Now, when a buyer contacts you for the headset, they will pay you $150 – you will take $100 and send to the supplier of the product who will then ship the headset directly to the buyer. Your own gain or profit in the entire transaction will be $50.

Dropshipping is a risk-free business model, and that's one of the reasons why anybody that wants to go into e-commerce is advised to start with dropshipping. Dropshipping is risk-free in that you don't get to handle the products you are selling – you are only a middleman or intermediary between the buyer of a product and a supplier of the same product.

Additionally, since you don't keep the inventory of the products you are selling, the risk that is associated with stock keeping has already been lifted off your shoulder. With minimal risks, you stand to gain more while doing minimal work. Furthermore, you don't have to be the one that develops the product you sell. One of the hardest parts of being an e-commerce entrepreneur is product research and development.

Many businesses fail because they did not do proper product research and development. However, as a dropshipper, you don't have to bother yourself with such burdens. The supplier of the product has already done a good job of researching and developing a hot-selling product. Your only job is to connect this supplier to a buyer of their product.

If one supplier stops making good products or if you find out about cheaper alternatives, you could switch suppliers, and your business will not be affected in any way. Many suppliers are happy to work with dropshippers because they (dropshippers) help them to grow their business and increase their customer reach. Some suppliers are even happy to stamp your name or company name on the product to make it seem as if you own the product.

That being said, dropshipping a win-win for all the parties involved. It is a win for you the dropshipper because you get to sell products that you don't manufacture and make money while at it. It is an easy way to make money online, and if done well, it can make you rich. Remember, e-commerce will continue to grow in the coming years. And as more and more people embrace e-commerce, your dropshipping business will continue to grow.

Dropshipping is a win for the customer or buyer because the products they buy through this means help them to solve their problems. When many people have issues or when they need products, they often do not know where or how to get the products. If a dropshipper helps such a buyer to find the products they need, then the buyer has benefited from dropshipping as a business model.

Besides, dropshipping is a win for the supplier of a product because dropshippers help them to sell more products. Think of this – if you are a supplier of a product, which would you prefer – to work with dropshippers and sell more or to shun dropshippers and sell less? Every smart business owner/supplier understands that it is better for them to partner with others and earn 50% than not to partner up and earn 0%. So, it is safe to say that dropshipping also helps suppliers to sell more products.

Why can't the buyer source products directly?

One of the commonest questions that people ask when they hear of dropshipping is, "why can't the buyer just source their products directly from the supplier?" While that is a logical question that anyone should ask, there are real reasons why buyers do not source for a product directly from a supplier. One of the reasons is that most buyers prefer to sit in the comfort of their bedroom and order the products they need.

Think of it this way – how many times do you go directly to a farm to source for your groceries? Even though going to the farm to source for supplies will cost less, and you are guaranteed of getting only fresh farm produce, many people still prefer to get their supplies from the grocery store. This is despite the fact that grocery stores sell at a far costlier price than what would be attainable in a farm. Also, before the products get to the grocery stores, they may already be losing their freshness, yet most people prefer to buy from the grocery stores. Why is that so?

The simple answer is convenience. We live in a fast-paced world where people want things instantly. That's why we have instant noodles, instant this and that. Everything is instant – no buyer wants to go through the rigorous stress of finding a direct supplier for a product that they want to buy. Rather, they choose to pay a little more for someone to do the job for them.

So, instead of sacrificing their comfort to look for a supplier, many online shoppers prefer to spare a few dollars to have someone else do it for them, and that's one of the reasons why dropshipping is booming and will continue to remain relevant in the coming years.

Even if a buyer decides to go scout for a product directly, they might just give up after a few tries. The reason is – even though the internet has made the world a global village, the truth still remains that it takes a special skill for someone to search and find desired products even on the internet. Going through many sources searching for a product can be time-consuming and tiring, and many online shoppers do not have that energy and time.

Another reason why online shoppers don't approach the suppliers directly is that they do not even know that an e-commerce store is a dropshipping store. A typical dropshipping store is just designed to look like your standard e-commerce store. There is no difference – when you get to the store, you see different products listed there with their individual prices. Then you also see an "order" button or instructions on how to order for the desired product.

On the surface, everything looks like a typical online store – then after the online shopper has ordered a product, the dropshipper does the rest of the job at the background or behind the scenes. The dropshipper will take the money paid by the online shopper and place an order on the website of the supplier. Then the supplier will fulfill the order and send the ordered product to the address of the online shopper. So, the online shopper does not even know that the online store they are ordering their product from is only but a dropshipping store.

We could summarize the reasons why online shoppers don't buy from a supplier directly as follows:

- Dropshipping makes the buying process easier for an online shopper.
- Many online shoppers don't know that they are buying from a dropshipper. They just want to have their ordered product delivered to their doorstep, and it does not matter if they pay a little more.
- In many cases, the online shopper has gotten to trust the dropshipping store, and won't want to trade with another brand that is yet to be tested and trusted. It is often said that the devil you know is better than the angel you don't know.

That being said, it is interesting to note that most of the independent online stores you come across on the internet are actually dropshipping stores. At the surface level, you would never know that such stores have dropshippers behind them. When you place an order for a product, dropshipping is then done behind the scene. Even on popular e-commerce marketplaces like Amazon, eBay, there are dropshipping stores there.

These popular marketplaces allow independent vendors to open stores on the platform – so, dropshippers also open their stores on there. If you have ever bought a product from Amazon or any of the other popular e-commerce marketplaces, then there is a high chance that the product was drop shipped. All this goes to show that dropshipping is more pervasive than you think – so starting a dropshipping store could never be a wrong business decision.

If you plan to run a successful dropshipping store, you don't need to spend a lot of money. However, you need to be a good researcher – this will help you to research and find hot-selling products which you can list on your store and make more money. Dropshipping business thrives on large volume sales – since the profit margins can be small sometimes, you need to sell in large volumes if you intend to make more money. This is one of the reasons why you need to research and come up with hot-selling products. You also need to design your store to be catchy enough and put SEO (Search Engine Optimization) into consideration when designing the store. We shall get to talk more on these tips in a later section of this guide.

Three ways to run a functional dropshipping store

There are two main popular ways to run a dropshipping store and one unpopular approach – let's talk about the three of them briefly. The first method or approach is to create a storefront on any of the popular e-commerce platforms. Once you have created the store, you need to research and find hot selling products and then list them on the store. When people order the product, you send their information across to a supplier to fulfill the order for you.

One advantage of having your dropshipping store on already established marketplaces is that you get to leverage the brand image of the e-commerce platform to sell more. Online shoppers already have a good perception of the major online ecom marketplaces. So, once you have a store on such marketplaces, the brand image rubs off on you. This means that a buyer would be more than likely to purchase from you.

For instance, Amazon is a well-recognized e-commerce marketplace – the platform is also well known for its customer satisfaction policy. Now, if you create a dropshipping storefront on Amazon, an online shopper will trust your store just for the mere fact that it is on Amazon or that it has Amazon's branding on it.

The role that branding or brand image plays in the success of a business can never be underestimated. So, if your store has a positive brand image as a result of its association with Amazon (associative branding), then you are sure to gain the trust of your potential buyers and record more sales.

Another advantage of having your dropshipping storefront on established e-commerce marketplaces is that you get to enjoy the enormous traffic that gets to such platforms daily. There is no doubt that platforms like Amazon welcome a barrage of human traffic every day. And all those visitors are on the platform for one thing – which is to buy something. If you position your store before such a vast audience, then you are sure to record sales.

With the type of traffic that gets to the platforms, you may not need to spend huge amounts of money on advertising your products or store. Yes, you may still need to pay some money to the different platforms for improved visibility, but that would be significantly lower than the amount you would have spent on PPC (Pay per Click) advertising, for instance, if you were trying to pull your own traffic to the store.

The only disadvantage or rather drawback that comes with selling on popular e-commerce marketplace is that the competition can be stifling. Since it is pretty easy to create a storefront on those platforms, the competition is quite high as there are many vendors jostling for the traffic that comes to the sites.

However, it is essential to note that competition is a normal part of running a business. There is no type of business that does not face competition, but your ability to position yours uniquely is what will differentiate your store from the millions of others that are available.

Another way through which you could run a dropshipping store is to create your own independent online store and then connect it to an order fulfillment platform like Shopify. To go with this approach, you will have to buy a domain name, hosting package, and then design your store from scratch. After designing the store, you will then populate it with products. Some plug-ins allow you to automatically import products from various order fulfillment sites into your own online store. Using such plug-ins or software applications will make the job of populating your store with as many products as possible easy for you.

Note: as a dropshipper, it is essential for you to add as many products as possible to your store. The more products you add, the more your sales. Remember, we said earlier that dropshipping thrives on volume sales. Since you are not even the person fulfilling the orders, you don't have to bother about the stress of fulfilling many orders at once.

The major advantage of creating your own independent dropshipping store is that you are entirely in charge of your business. If you create a store on a popular marketplace like Amazon or eBay, you could wake up one morning to find that your store has been deleted or restricted. If another company can delete or restrict your business, then it is safe to say that you don't have a business. Running your own independent store puts you in control. You decide the types of products you want to list on your store and those you don't want.

A significant disadvantage of running an independent store is that you would have to do your own branding yourself. Getting prospects to trust your store and leave their money with you can be a hard task. You will work extra hard before you could gain the trust of your audience. This is unlike what happens when you are selling on a popular marketplace – the brand image of the marketplace serves as an umbrella that covers you.

Another disadvantage of running your own independent dropshipping store is that you will have to spend a lot of money on marketing. You will be responsible for driving traffic to your store, and this can often be expensive. Running PPC campaigns all the time can take a huge toll on your income and reduce your profit significantly. And unless your store has become very popular, you will always need to run ads for people to keep coming to your store.

The third, albeit unconventional method to run a dropshipping store, is the social media approach. This involves showcasing high in demand products on social media – when your followers or other social media users like any of the products you have displayed, they would order them. You will then need to source for a supplier who will deliver the product to the online shopper.

This type of dropshipping could best be described as manual dropshipping although some people would choose to call it retail arbitrage. Many dropshippers usually start their journey on social media and then proceed to build their own platforms or create stores on e-commerce marketplaces.

One major advantage of this dropshipping approach is that it is the least expensive option. You don't pay any money to create a post on social media. It is also easy – you are not required to set up anything. Any regular social media user can create posts and ask people interested in a product to get in touch.

A major disadvantage is that you will have to gain the trust of your followers first before they are willing to do business with you – and this can take time. Also, you will need to grow a large social media following – again; this can take time. If you want to work with social media influencers (people with large social media following), you will have to spend a lot of money.

Another disadvantage is that your business will be at the mercy of the social media platform in question. The social media platform that you are using could decide to restrict the number of your followers who get to see your ad posts. If that happens, you will have to run PPC campaigns, which can be quite expensive.

Often, people who are new to dropshipping do ask, "Which is of the three approaches is best for a newbie?" There is no straightforward answer to that question – some dropshippers start with social media while others start with e-commerce marketplaces. It depends on you and the level of technical knowledge you have. You could even start with your own independent store if you are sure of what you are doing.

Since we have looked at the different ways of running a dropshipping store, let's proceed to talk about how to actually create and run one. But before then, let's summarize some of the reasons why dropshipping is excellent for every e-commerce entrepreneur.

Why bother about dropshipping?

Here are a few reasons why you should consider starting your own dropshipping business today:

1. It is easy to start

As mentioned earlier, starting a new business used to be hard – however, business models like dropshipping have made owning a business a simple process. As a dropshipper, you don't need to worry about getting office space; you don't have to worry about hiring and paying staff; at least when you are just starting. You may need to hire virtual assistants to assist in running the business later, but that's when you have grown to a reasonable extent.

Furthermore, you don't have to bother about securing huge startup capital – essentially, you are not using your money to run the business. You are only but a middle man, you take money from an online shopper, pay some of the money to a supplier of a product, and you keep the remaining as your profit. So, you don't need huge funds — if you already have a computer or even a mobile phone and an internet connection, then you could start and grow a dropshipping store.

Since you don't fulfill your own orders yourself, you don't have to worry about product research and development. The product's supplier has already done an excellent job of researching and developing the right product so that the burden is no longer on you. If a product stops selling well, you will only need to research and find other hot-selling products and list them on your store. As you may already know, product research and development is one of the most challenging aspects of running a business. But as a dropshipper, that aspect is already taken care of. So, you are hugely in luck.

Once you have found a good product that you want to sell, you only need a platform to display them or make them visible to buyers. You could leverage existing and already trusted e-commerce marketplaces to display your products, or you could create your own independent online store. Social media is also a great place for displaying the products you are selling.

2. Easy access to millions of products

As a dropshipper, you could list thousands of products on your store and make more money. The more products you list, the more your chances of recording sales, which translates to more money for you. Listing as much as a thousand products on your store is practicable since you are not the one developing the products or fulfilling the orders.

You are not restricted to one type of product – you could source for products from different suppliers and list them on your store. Whenever a product is ordered, you simply send the order details to the affected supplier to fulfill the order. To list different products, you just need to create different sections on your store, especially if it is an independent store.

For instance, you could list headphones, totem bags, phone cases, belts, shoes, etc. on the same dropshipping store.

3. You can set the price of products

A supplier will often give you products at wholesale or reduced prices – you could then add your own profit to the cost and sell to the buyer. If you desire to make more money, you could raise your prices slightly while ensuring it is still reasonable.

4. Easily scalable

As a dropshipper, you can easily scale up your business by hiring virtual assistants to assist in the running of the business. You could also create more stores on other marketplaces where you don't have one already. You could research and list more products to increase your profitability.

Downsides

Dropshipping has its own downsides – so, it is essential that we also mention some of them. Without romanticizing everything, here are some of the disadvantages of dropshipping:

1. High competition

If you have a store on any of the popular e-commerce marketplaces, which is what most dropshippers do, then you will have to deal with stiff competition. Dropshipping has a very low barrier of entry – it is a business which anybody can join – and as expected, the competition is very high. However, you could always overcome competition by developing unique strategies. And you have to understand that there is competition in every business. Even those businesses that have a very high barrier of entry still face competition.

So, you have to see competition as a regular thing in business and work out strategies on how to stand out from the crowd. The best way to beat the competition in dropshipping is to find and sell unique products that many people are not already selling. Most dropshippers have a herd mentality – once they hear that one item is selling like hotcakes, they will all rush in to sell the same product. Do not be like most dropshippers; you should be different if you ever want to stand way above the competition.

2. Supplier error

Sometimes, you order a different thing, and the supplier sends an entirely different item to your buyer. This happens more often – and in such situations, the buyer might escalate the situation and hurt your business. Supplier error can make you lose money as you will need to use your money to pay for the actual product that the buyer wanted.

3. Shipping times are usually longer

Most suppliers are based in distant countries like China – as a result, ordered products will often take a longer time to get to the buyer. While many buyers do not care about long shipping times, some others will not take it. Some potential buyers will not purchase from your store if they discover that the shipping time will be longer than necessary – making you lose out on money you would have made.

The above are just some of the downsides of running a dropshipping business. Despite these assume downsides, dropshipping is still a great business model for anyone who wants to become financially independent while keying into new global trends. If you are now convinced that dropshipping is for you, then read on as the next sections of this guide will take you by the hand and show you how to create and grow your own e-commerce empire.

Chapter Two:

Dropshipping on Shopify

In the previous section, I mentioned that you could create your own independent dropshipping store, add products, and then sell to your customers. You could also create a store on any of the popular e-commerce marketplaces and sell your products. Additionally, you could grow a massive following on social media and dropship products to them. We also saw some of the advantages and disadvantages of each of the options.

In this chapter, we are going to talk about how to create an independent dropshipping store using Shopify. This is going to be a step by step guide, covering everything you need to know about creating a store using Shopify. When you are done reading this chapter, you should know how to create your own Shopify store, customize it to your taste, and import products from aliexpress.com, one of the most popular Chinese e-commerce marketplaces, into your Shopify store.

You will also learn how to fulfill your orders, customize your product listings to make them unique and general tips on how to succeed as a Shopify e-commerce entrepreneur. Without further ado, let's dive in and start exploring the various options that Shopify present.

First things first – what is Shopify?

Shopify is a software tool which allows you to create an e-commerce website – it does not end at that, the tool has a shopping cart solution which you can use to create product listing, manage your listings and fulfill your orders. Shopify does not just allow you to create a website; it helps you turn the site into an online store.

What makes a website an online store? A website becomes an online store when the administrator of the site can create product listings and manage them on the site. Also, when users visit the store, they could be able to add desired products to a shopping cart, manage the items in their shopping cart and check out when they are done shopping. Shopify's shopping cart solution gives you all the tools to turn the website you will create using available themes into an online store.

Why do people prefer Shopify?

Shopify is an e-commerce management tool of choice for several reasons – one of the reasons is that it is easy to use. To create a store, you simply need to create an account, choose the desired theme, customize the theme, download all the necessary plug-ins, then add products, and start selling. It is as simple as that.

Creating an independent e-commerce website without using Shopify may be difficult for you. There are several things you will need to do to make that happen. However, with Shopify, most of the tools you need are already available. You only need to download the necessary plug-in that offers the functionality you need.

A plug-in is a piece of software that is designed to complement the functions of a bigger software tool. Most plug-ins are usually developed by third parties to perform added functions, ones not available in an already existing software solution. Shopify has a shopping cart solution; however, there are still some functionalities that the tool lacks.

Those missing functionalities can be replaced by plug-ins. For instance, Shopify originally doesn't have the functionality that allows you to import products directly from another e-commerce platform into your Shopify store. But a plug-in like Oberlo enables you to import products directly from aliexpress.com into your Shopify store. You can also use the plug-in to organize your products, manage your listings, modify or update product details, and perform a host of other exciting functions.

Another thing that makes Shopify great is that anyone from anywhere can use it. And most interestingly, the products you want to sell doesn't necessarily need to belong to you. You can fulfill orders both manually and automatically. Manual fulfillment of orders becomes an option when you have just a few listings, but if you work with third-party e-commerce platforms like aliexpress.com and you have a ton of products and a lot of orders as well, then automatic order fulfillment becomes a preferred option.

Some plug-ins help you to fulfill orders automatically – for instance, if you import your dropshipping products directly from aliexpress, the plug-in known as Oberlo can help you place orders on Aliexpress and fulfill the orders automatically. With such a plug-in, you only do little work and still earn money.

For Shopify, there are plug-ins for most functions you could think of, and these plug-ins all help to make your life as a dropshipper easier. We shall talk about these plug-ins in a subsequent section of this guide. With the right use of plug-ins, you could turn your Shopify store into a passive income spinner. This means you would just need to do little work, then go to bed and sleep while you keep making money. We shall talk about that later.

For all these features that Shopify has and the fantastic opportunities it offers, the tool is almost free. In fact, the price is just negligible, and when you start making money, you will not remember that you are paying a subscription fee for the tool. Furthermore, Shopify runs an affiliate program, which means that if you talk to people about Shopify and they get to register an account, you will earn an affiliate commission. The more people you talk to about the tool, the more the affiliate commission you will make.

So, if you have a massive audience of e-commerce enthusiasts, you could show them the fantastic functionalities of Shopify, then convince them to sign up, and when they do, you get to earn affiliate commissions. Now, if you add your earnings as an affiliate and your actual earnings from the sales of your dropshipping products, it means more money in your pocket. This is not a book on affiliate marketing; so I won't delve too deeply into the subject. I have a comprehensive book on affiliate marketing – if you would want to learn more about the topic, then consider getting the book.

Let's now talk about Shopify and how to create an e-commerce website using the tool. To create your own e-commerce website using Shopify and start selling dropshipping products in a few hours, here are the steps you need to take:

Step one: Start with a free Shopify store

Shopify, just like many other internet service providers allows you to start with a free account and then start paying for the tool when you are really convinced that dropshipping or e-commerce as a whole is for you. The truth is that if you follow the advice in this guide religiously, you will have no reason to abandon dropshipping. Dropshipping can be the channel you need to go through to become an e-commerce giant, and it starts with creating a free Shopify account.

Shopify understands that not everybody who creates an account will get to continue after the trial period. So, they give you a 14-day trial period to test the waters – if after the 14 days, and you are convinced that this is what you want to do, then you can start paying for the tool.

To create a Shopify account, you simply need to type www.shopify.com into your browser. On the homepage, click on "start free trial." you will be shown a registration form that will mandate you to enter your email address, password and store name. Enter your correct email address – this is important because a confirmation email will be sent to the email you provided. You will need to click on the link in the confirmation email to continue to create your store.

Additionally, you need to choose a password – and when doing that, do not forget to follow password creation guidelines. You would want to make your password a combination of upper and lower case letters. You also want to include numbers and special characters in the password. Don't worry about forgetting the password; you can always use the password recovery feature to reset the password.

Just like your other online accounts, it is important that you keep your password safe because if the password gets compromised, someone could gain access to your Shopify account and modify some things. For instance, an intruder could hijack your store and even change some vital details like your bank account information.

After choosing a secure password, enter your store name. It is important that you choose a unique store name – do not just enter the first word or phrase that comes to your head. Remember, you are trying to build a long term e-commerce business, and it all starts with the name you choose for your store.

Giving your store a random name means you only see it as a "hustle" or something you do because you want to raise quick money to pay your house rent or settle some urgent bills. If you really see e-commerce as a business of the future, then you would want to sit and think of a better name for your store.

Even if it would take you a few days to come up with a good name, then pause the registration until you have figured out a perfect name. The reason why it seems as if I am emphasizing on choosing a great name is that the name of your store forms part of your branding. What do you think differentiates

Apple phones from any other random phone out there?

The answer is branding! Your store name alone could make a customer decide not to buy from you. Remember, we still live in a world where people buy things based on emotions. Something as simple as a name could sway a potential buyer's emotions and make them not to buy from you.

Choose a name that depicts the types of products you want to sell. Also, make sure that the name is not too long. Ideally, shorter names that just consist of a single word are preferred. Names with two words are also great – you just need to ensure it is unique. In fact, if another store is already using your chosen name, Shopify will let you know and ask you to choose a different one.

Once you have entered a valid email, created a secure password, and entered your desired store name, then you are ready to create your first Shopify store. Next, click on "Create your store," and your store will be created by Shopify. This may take some time to be completed – you have to be patient and wait for Shopify to complete the process.

After your store has been created, a new page will come up requiring you to fill out some additional information about yourself. Filling out the information on this second page is not mandatory; if you don't feel comfortable doing it, you could simply skip it and go to the next page. Even though filling out this page is optional, you might want to do it anyway. For Shopify to include the page, they must have a tangible reason for doing that. However, if you don't want to fill out the information there, just click on "Next" and move on to the next page.

On the next page that comes up, you will be required to enter some personal information about yourself. For instance, you will be required to enter your personal information like your first name, last name, address, zip code, phone number, website (optional), etc. When you are done filling out the required information, click on "Enter my store," and Shopify will take you to your brand new Shopify store. Your account is fresh, with no products listed and no customizations. You need to get to work and customize the store and start listing products.

Important tip: when you make your first sale, Shopify will send your earnings to the email you used in opening your Shopify account. What this means is that if you used an email that is not already linked to or associated with any PayPal account, your money would remain in the email until you link it to a PayPal account before you receive your payout into your PayPal account.

Shopify uses PayPal as the default payment method – so when you are creating your Shopify account, at the point where you are asked to enter your email, it is important that you use an email address that is already linked to your personal PayPal account. As mentioned earlier, Shopify automatically assumes that the email you have used to create your Shopify account is linked to a PayPal merchant account – hence when you earn money, Shopify will send the money to the email you used in creating your account.

Now, if the email you used in creating your account is not linked to any PayPal account, you will need to create a PayPal account using the email so that Shopify can always process your payments into the email. Otherwise, your payouts will keep hanging in the email until you link it to a PayPal account.

After creating your store, the next thing you want to do is to choose a theme, customize it, and start adding products to the store. That takes us to step two, which is theme customization.

Step Two: Choose a Shopify theme

A theme is simply the overall style, feel, and look of your Shopify store. It shows how your products will be displayed in your store. It also shows how the various layouts and components of the store will be positioned. Without a theme, you would have to do a manual design of the layout, style, and outlook of your website. With a theme to the rescue, you only need to do a small job of customizing what is already there.

You have two options when it comes to choosing a theme for your Shopify store – you could decide to buy a theme from a third-party vendor or buy directly from Shopify. One disadvantage of buying from a third party vendor is that Shopify may not approve the theme. Shopify prefers that themes used on the platform should be mobile responsive and user-friendly as well. If Shopify feels that the theme you got from a third party doesn't meet those requirements, the theme could be rejected.

Normally, you don't need to even go to a third party to buy a theme for your Shopify store. Shopify's theme store has a wide variety of themes you can choose from. If you choose a theme from Shopify itself, you won't worry about having it approved or not.

To get to Shopify's theme store, simply click on "Themes" on your Shopify dashboard. If you don't want to use that option, you can visit the theme store directly by clicking on https://themes.shopify.com. As the name suggests, it is a theme store where you can find thousands of themes you can use to customize your Shopify store.

You will find two types of themes on Shopify's theme store – you will find free themes and paid ones. The cheapskate in you would want you to just pick a random free theme and run along. However, you need to understand that e-commerce is serious business, and if you want it to pay you like a business, you must treat it as a business. If, on the other hand, you treat it like a hobby, it will pay you like a hobby. That being said, one of the primary ways to know that you are treating your e-commerce or dropshipping business as a hobby is when you decide to go for free themes.

Dropshipping using Shopify is a business that will make you money, and for something that has such potential, you need to invest money into it. One reason why many people don't often want to invest in their dropshipping business is that they were sold a lie. They were told that you could start a dropshipping business without capital. While it is true that you can do dropshipping business with little money since you are not purchasing any products directly; you still need a little money to set up the business and run marketing campaigns to attract customers.

That being said, you are better off with a paid theme. Even the layout of the free themes should send a signal to you that says, "This is not what I want for my business." Paid themes look more professional, inviting, and user-friendly. With such a user-friendly theme, converting your store visitors to actual customers will not be a hard task for you.

Imagine that you have spent a lot of money running PPC campaigns and then the potential customer gets to your store, heaves a sigh, and clicks away, how would that make you feel? Do not forget – people buy things based on emotions. Someone could just decide to buy from you because they love the color or layout of your store. Some people could decide to buy based on the sleekness of the store while others could decide to buy from you based on how fast your site loads. So, it is not ideal for you to lose customers because of something that is within your control.

Different themes come at different prices – some sell for $180 while others sell for $160. The price of a theme depends on so many factors – for instance, its layout, color schemes, and most importantly, the industry it is designed for.

You also need to consider your industry when choosing a theme – some themes are best suited for some industries than others. For instance, if you want to sell clothing items, then you must select a theme that is for the beauty or fashion industry.

Apart from the above considerations, here are some other things you need to factor in when choosing a Shopify theme:

1. Aesthetics

Before choosing a theme, consider its aesthetics, its feel, and how it blends with your industry and brand. A common mistake that most dropshippers, especially beginners, make when they want to choose a theme is that they go for the ones that suit their taste. Yes, it is good to look for a theme that you think is nice; however, an important fact you should always keep in mind is that you are not designing your e-commerce store for yourself. Yes, you heard that right – the store belongs to you, but you are not serving yourself. Your store serves your customers – so it is safe to say that the store belongs to your customers.

Since the store is not for you but for your customers, you should design it to appeal to them. One way to know what would appeal to your customers is to consider your industry and ask yourself relevant questions. Ask yourself a question like, "What color scheme would someone in the fashion industry like?" "What theme would appeal to someone in the healthcare industry?" Once you ask the relevant questions and get your answers, then you are sure to understand what your customer would like.

Themes come with pre designed elements which you can replace with your own materials. Before you choose a theme, check out the layouts, design, and be sure that what you have will fit into the theme's layout and elements.

2. Think about your logo

Remember, your e-commerce store is like your typical offline business – if you are running an offline business, you would want to ensure that you get your branding right. Before even creating a store, make sure you have gotten the branding of your e-commerce business right. For instance, make sure you have chosen a name – this should be the same name you will use as your store name. Additionally, make sure you have designed a logo. This logo will appear on your branding materials and marketing materials. The logo will appear on your website, social media pages, and every other place where you market your e-commerce business.

Since your logo will appear on your store, you need to be sure that the theme you want to choose will accommodate the logo well. Every theme has a logo placeholder, where your logo will fit in. Check and ensure that your logo will fit into the provided placeholder. If the available placeholder makes the logo look odd, then consider choosing another theme.

Also, you need to be sure that the color scheme of the logo matches that of the theme – you don't want the colors on your e-commerce store to riot with each other. Remember, it is the simplest of things that often turn off customers. You might think that it is not necessary, but a logo that looks out of place could spell unprofessionalism, and customers don't want to deal with such vendors or merchants.

3. Think content

Every theme comes pre designed with layouts and content. You will only need to replace the available content, design, graphics, and images with your own. Now, look at the layout, content, and images available on the theme and ask yourself, "Will my content, images, graphics, etc. fit into the available placeholders without the content spilling over?" If the content you have wouldn't fit into the available layouts perfectly, then consider another theme.

For instance, if a theme has heavy images and lengthy texts, but your store is meant to contain only a few images and very few texts, then you don't want to consider such a theme. You have to look further until you find a theme that fits the type of store or design you have in mind.

4. Will the theme accommodate the types of products you have?

If the products you sell fall under many categories and subcategories, will the theme accommodate those categories? This is one important question you should ask yourself. If the theme cannot contain all the categories of items you want to sell, then you might have problems fitting all your products into the theme.

A theme will have some expanding menu that helps you put your products under different categories. If the theme you want only allows for 50 categories, whereas your products will be classified into 30 categories, then you should not choose that theme. In the same vein, if your store has 50 categories and the theme's expanding menu or dropdown menu only allows for 30 categories, you should also look elsewhere.

You want a theme that will accommodate all the different categories of products that you would want to sell. This is important for many reasons – one; it helps you maintain a clean looking store where items are not spilling over each other. Secondly, it helps your customer locate the items they want in the right categories.

Many customers don't have the time nor patience to start looking for the products they want. Once they look for the product in the category where it is supposed to appear, and it is not there, they automatically assume that you don't have the product and look elsewhere. You should never allow avoidable mistakes to make you lose customers.

5. Can you get support?

All the themes available on the Shopify theme store were developed by third party software developers and placed on the platform for sale. While the themes are being made available to you by Shopify, it is not the responsibility of Shopify to ensure that you get support from the developers of the theme when the need arises.

Something could go wrong when you are trying to install your Shopify theme, and you might need to get in touch with the support team of the developers for help. Before settling for a theme, make sure you will be able to get support when necessary.

The best way to know that the developers of a theme offer support is to look at what other dropshippers or e-commerce entrepreneurs have said about the theme and its developers. The themes available on the theme store are showcased like your typical products on a typical e-commerce store. You will see a sample of the theme and how it looks, you will see its price, and you will also see reviews that other people have left about the theme and its support team.

Go through the reviews and see the common complaints that people have made about the theme. As always, you are advised to leave out the shiny five-star reviews – but you could still look at them, especially if they don't appear to be too good to be true. You might also want to leave out the "one-word reviews." One-word reviews include those that just say, "Nice theme." Such reviews are not explicit enough to tell you what are the problems common with the theme or what makes the theme great. Look for the three stars and two stars reviews. Often, those are the most honest reviews.

When going through the reviews, watch out to see if a reviewer would comment about the availability of the development theme to offer support when needed. If a lot of people complained that they were not able to get support when they needed it, then you might want to consider looking for another good theme.

Often, developers of a theme leave their contact information in the description box of the theme. Don't be shy to contact them to ask relevant questions before finally committing your money. Remember, you are paying for the theme, so it is your right to get all the information you need before making the final commitment.

Now that you have gotten yourself a suitable theme, it is time to customize it and start uploading products to your store.

Customizing your Shopify store's theme

Remember, a theme is just a designed layout that contains several placeholders which you will need to customize to make it yours. Theme designers normally create placeholders with generic texts and images which you need to replace with your own texts and the images of your products. Customizing a theme is as easy as ABC – with an available drag and drop feature, all you need to do is drag your own texts and images into the available placeholders, and you are good to go.

The image below shows the skeleton of a theme. The theme has been stripped of the images and texts.

As you can see from the above image, there is a placeholder for your business name, which in this case is your store name. There is also a placeholder for your logo – you need to fill out those placeholders with your correct data.

Here are some of the things you need to change in your new Shopify theme:

- Change the random generic logo on the theme and replace it with yours

- Change the generic business name on the theme and replace it with your store name

- If you don't like the background color of the theme, you can simply replace it. You are often advised to go for a theme that already has the color scheme you desire so that you don't have to start changing color all over again.

- You can change the font if you don't like the default fonts – you can increase or reduce the font size, font style, and font name if you desire.

- The navigation menus will obviously contain generic text; you are to replace that with your own custom texts. If the texts of the navigation menus and boxes are the same with what you already have in mind, then there is no need to change them again.

- If there are areas, layouts, or elements on the theme you don't need, you can remove them.

- If you intend to grow an email list, you can add your link or subscribe form to the theme. If you don't want to start building an email list just yet, simply hide the newsletter layout until you are ready to start using it.

Other things you can adjust on the theme include the following:

- The labels of the categories and subcategories

- The large featured images on the homepage of the theme

- Links to social media pages

- The texts that appear on information pages. Information pages include "about us," "policy pages," "contact us," and all those other similar pages.

- As you already know, you can add or remove product listings

- Information that appears on the header and footer of the theme.

Since this is not a book on theme customization, we shall not go deep into how to perform the above functions. You can find books or even videos on how to do any of the things listed above. If you a perfect DIYer, you can modify the theme without consulting any source – it is simple, and the "drag and drop" feature available to you makes everything even simpler.

Once you are done customizing your theme, adding everything that needs to be added – next, you want to start uploading products to your store. Normally, if you are the owner of the products you want to sell, you would do the manual addition of products. Even as a dropshipper, you can still do manual product listing – however, seeing as you will be uploading hundreds of products, you will need to install a plug-in that helps you automate product listing.

To list a product is just a simple process – but for you to understand what it involves, let's look at what you will find when you visit a typical e-commerce store. When you get to an e-commerce store, you will find hundreds, if not thousands of products on display. If you click on one of the products, you will be taken directly to the offer page of that particular listing or product. On the offer image, you will see a clearer picture of the product, its description (which is basically a description of its features), the price of the product and a button that says, "Add to cart."

Now, if you want to list a product, you simply need to upload photos of the product, write something to describe the product, state the price of the product, and you are done. For the checkout button, it is added automatically by the e-commerce platform you are using – in this case, Shopify. If the product goes out of stock, the order now or "add to cart" button changes to "out of stock." Shopify does all of that for you – that's why it is called a shopping cart solution or tool.

As an e-commerce entrepreneur who just wants to add ten original products they own – the product listing process will be so easy for you. You only need to take photos of the product, write the product descriptions and you are good to go.

Just imagine that you are a dropshipper who wants to add close to hundred products from other e-commerce marketplaces into your Shopify store, how are you going to get that tedious job done? Will you have to keep uploading the details of the products one after the day until you get to the hundredth product? Of course, that will be a cumbersome process – you will need a tool to make the job easier. You will need a plug-in that can automatically import your desired products into your Shopify store.

Step Three: Install Oberlo

Oberlo is a powerful plug-in that makes the job of importing products into your Shopify store easy and straightforward. Oberlo is specifically designed to work with aliexpress.com and Shopify – if you install the plugin, you will be able to import products directly from the Aliexpress website into your Shopify store. Most dropshippers who get their products from aliexpress.com suppliers make use of Oberlo to import products and fulfill orders automatically.

Here are some of the reasons why Oberlo is such a great plug-in:

1. It helps you to easily add products to your store – with Oberlo; you don't need to add or list products manually. The tool helps you to import products directly from Aliexpress into your Shopify store. All you need is to indicate some of the products you want and click a button; then the tool uploads the

same products into your store with the same product images, description, etc. You might consider changing some of the product's details before finally importing them.

2. You can change suppliers easily as you desire – if a particular supplier stops performing well, you can change suppliers using Oberlo – and the process is such an easy one.

3. Oberlo automatically manages your inventory – what is inventory management? This involves the supervision of the products you have listed in your store to know when they are in stock and when they are out of stock. Since you are using suppliers on aliexpress.com to fulfill your orders – what Oberlo does is that it monitors aliexpress.com so that if any product you have in your store goes out of stock on aliexpress.com, Oberlo automatically changes the status of the product to "out of stock" on your website as well.

It is necessary that Oberlo does this automatic stock inventory because you don't want the status of a product to state "in stock" on your e-commerce website whereas it is out of stock on aliexpress.com. If a customer orders a product from your store because it is showing "in stock" and the product turns out to be out of stock on aliexpress, you may have a hard time fulfilling the order.

Oberlo also updates the price of the products you have listed on your site automatically. The plug-in is always crawling aliexpress.com to see that the prices of the products you listed on your Shopify store have not changed on aliexpress.com.

Let's assume that you are selling phone cases and you initially listed the price as $50 on your Shopify store. If the price of the product changes to $60, for instance, on aliexpress.com, Oberlo will automatically update the price of the product on your store. That is, Oberlo will change the price of the product in your store from $50 to $60. This automatic price update is important as it saves you from making a loss.

Imagine that the price of a product has increased on aliexpress.com and you listed the product at a lower price in your store, it means that when customers order the product, you will use your own money to make up for the difference. You don't want to start telling a customer that you listed the wrong price. That would spell unprofessionalism and show that you are not serious with your business. Such a customer might choose to cancel their orders with you, and that would mark the end of their business relationship with you. The customer could proceed to write scathing reviews about you and your business on your social media pages, and that would likely drive away potential customers.

Oberlo helps take the stress of monitoring your listings and updating them manually away from you. As said earlier, if a product goes out of stock on aliexpress.com, the tool marks the product as out of stock on your site. If the price of the product you have listed changes on aliexpress.com, Oberlo updates the price of the product on your site automatically.

4. You can use it to customize your product before listing – normally, you can import products with all of its attributes (product image, product description, etc.) directly from aliexpress.com into your Shopify store. But sometimes, the product might have a photo which you don't want, or you would want to change. Also, the product's description might look too unappealing to you, and you might want to change it. With Oberlo, you can do all the customizations you want to do before importing the products into your Shopify store.

5. Automated pricing – this is part of the automatic inventory management that Shopify helps you to do. As explained earlier, one of the beauties of Oberlo is that if the price of a product changes on aliexpress.com, the plug-in automatically updates

the cost of the product in your store to match that on aliexpress.com.

6. Automatic order fulfillment – when you use aliexpress.com suppliers, and you get an order, what you do is to order the product from aliexpress.com supplier and then ship to your customer. This might be an easy thing to do when you get about 3 to 5 orders in a day. What happens if you have close to 50 or even 100 orders in a day, how do you handle all of that manually?

Oberlo takes the burden of order fulfillment off your shoulders. Once you get an order on your site, Oberlo takes over, places an order for the product on aliexpress.com and provide the shipping address of the customer. Oberlo also tracks the orders and provides tracking details to your customer. You can also follow the tracking details that Oberlo provides you until the product arrives at its destination.

7. Track your sales – Oberlo helps you to track and record your sales so that you know how your store is performing. Without properly tracking your sales, you will not know if you are making profits or losses. You can look at your sales history over a given period to see if you have been making progress or if you have been doing poorly. With the sales report, you can modify your strategies if need be or stick to your current strategies.

In addition to the above benefits of Oberlo, you can also run multiple user accounts. This means that if you have more than one Shopify store, you can create another user dedicated to your second store on the same Shopify account.

Oberlo is the plug-in of choice for most Shopify users because of the many benefits it has. The only assumed problem that Oberlo has is that it is specifically built for Shopify. If your dropshipping store is built using WordPress, for instance, then you cannot use Oberlo. But there are also alternatives to Oberlo which you can use on WordPress – a good example is Alidropship. Alidropship is a plug-in that works just like Oberlo – what it does is that it converts your WordPress website into a functional dropshipping store.

Now that we have looked at some of the benefits of Oberlo; let's proceed to talk about how to install it on your Shopify store.

Installing Oberlo

As mentioned earlier, Oberlo is a Shopify plug-in which also has a Google Chrome extension – you have to install the extension on your Google Chrome browser. To install Oberlo, visit app.oberlo.com, then click on the signup. After you have signed up, you will be taken to your dashboard – on your dashboard; you will see instructions on how to link your Shopify store to your Oberlo account. The instructions are pretty straightforward – just follow it and link your store to the Oberlo app.

You will be needed to grant Oberlo some permissions to manage your Shopify store. Once you have done that, you will be able to install the Oberlo app on your Shopify account. After linking your store, the next thing you want to do is to install the Oberlo extension on your browser.

The job of the Oberlo Chrome browser extension is to make the job of importing products into your store easy. When you have installed the extension, you just need to click a button to be able to import products directly from aliexpress.com into your Shopify store. If you don't have the Google Chrome browser, then you will need to download and install it at this point. Chrome browser is free – so you don't have to pay money to use.

After installing Google Chrome, simply type "Oberlo Chrome extension" into your search bar. The first result that Google will pop out will lead you directly to the download page of the Oberlo Chrome extension. Download and install the extension on your Google Chrome browser, and you are good to go.

Once you have installed the extension, look at the top right-hand corner of your browser, you will see the Oberlo icon there. If you see the icon, then it means that the extension was installed successfully. If you don't see the icon, then you might want to reinstall the extension or activate it.

With your Oberlo account created and linked to your Shopify store and with your Oberlo Chrome extension properly installed, everything is now set for you to start importing products from aliexpress.com into your Shopify store using the Oberlo app.

Step four: Importing products into your store

To import products from aliexpress.com into your Shopify store, you will need to use your Chrome browser. Your Chrome browser is where your Oberlo browser extension installed. So, you need to use it to make the process of product importation easy.

Open your browser and type www.aliexpress.com into the address box. You will be taken directly to the Aliexpress website. You will find some products on the homepage, but they may not be the exact products you want to import into your store. Remember, before getting to this stage; you must have carried out in-depth product research to know the exact types of products that do well and those you would want to avoid.

You have two options when it comes to finding the products you want on aliexpress.com. One, you could simply browse through the different categories, locate the category for the product you want to import and proceed to look for the exact product.

Another approach is to just type the keywords for the product or the name of the product if you know it into the search bar. You will see a lot of results. When you have found the product you want to import, how do you continue the process?

Simply hover your mouse over the product of interest or place your mouse over the listing and the Oberlo icon will appear on the listing. This is why you need to use a browser that has the Oberlo extension installed. If the Oberlo extension is not installed on your browser, the Oberlo icon, which you will click to import products into your Shopify store will not appear.

If you have found the particular product you want to import, and you have placed your mouse over the product listing, you will see the Oberlo icon. Click on the icon, and you will get a confirmation message that shows that you have successfully imported the product into your Shopify store.

See the image below for clarification.

In the above image, I tried to import the second product into my Shopify store, so, I placed my mouse over it. You can see that the Oberlo icon only appeared by the side of the listing because it is the only product of interest to me. Remember, I am only using this as an example.

Now, if I click on the icon, I will get a notification message that shows that I have successfully imported the product.

The image below shows the notification message you will get when a product has been successfully imported.

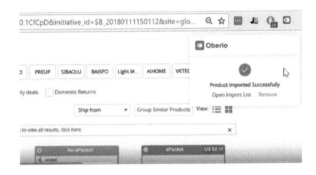

As you can see from the image, you can open your "import list" and see all the products you have imported. You can also remove some products and add others as much as you want.

If you want to add more products to your import list, you simply need to repeat the above process. First, search for the product or go through the different browse categories to find the product. When you have seen the product, hover your mouse over it, and the Oberlo icon will appear. Click on the icon and add the product to your import list.

Earlier, we mentioned that one of the advantages of using Oberlo is that it lets you modify or edit the products you have imported before you finally add them to your Shopify store. Once you have added all the products you want to import to Oberlo import list, click on "open import list" button. See the image above for clarification.

When you open the import list, you will see all the products you have imported. You can change the product description of any of them. You can also change the product photo by uploading your own custom photo. Sometimes, the product images of some products on aliexpress.com may not be clear enough – so you might want to change some of them.

An important detail you will definitely want to change is the price of the product. You want to make a profit – which means that the price you list a product on your Shopify store must be higher than the price of the product on aliexpress.com.

For example, if a product is selling for $40 on aliexpress.com, you might want to list the product for $50 on your store. Anytime the product is bought, you will make a profit of $10, which is fair enough since you are not the one fulfilling the order yourself.

You have to be sure that you are giving your products reasonable prices – remember that the dropshipping space is super competitive. High prices could chase your potential customers away, and low prices can lower your profit margins. You need to find a balance – if possible, search for other stores and see how much they are selling similar products.

Once you are done editing all the details you want to change – description, image, price, etc., then click on "save" and all the products you have added to Oberlo import list will automatically be imported into your Shopify store. Visit your Shopify store, and you will find the products being displayed there.

Notice how the Oberlo app makes the process of adding listings to your Shopify store as simple as ABC. You just have to click a button, and your preferred product will be moved from aliexpress.com into your Shopify store. With the Oberlo app, you can import as much as 50 products at once. If you want to do that manually, you may end up spending a whole day to upload just 10 products.

After importing products to your store, then it is time for you to go on aggressive marketing and watch orders start rolling in. In a subsequent section of this guide, we shall talk about some of the marketing methods you can use to drive traffic and potential buyers to your Shopify store.

Step five: Enable payment gateways

When you make money from your store, you will be paid through PayPal. We mentioned this earlier when we said you need to make sure that the email you use in opening your Shopify account is linked to a PayPal account.

If the email used in opening your Shopify account is linked to a PayPal, Shopify will be exiting your payments to your PayPal via the email. However, if the email is not linked to any PayPal account, you need to create a PayPal account using the email; otherwise, your payments will be stuck until do so.

If you don't want to receive your payments through PayPal, you could consider setting up Shopify payments which you will use to receive the money you made selling on Shopify store. When you set up Shopify Payments, Shopify will send your earnings directly into your bank account.

To set up Shopify payments, go to your Shopify dashboard and click on "Settings" at the bottom left side of the page. Click on "Payment Providers" and proceed to click on "Complete account setup" under Shopify payments. Next, add your bank account details so that you can start receiving your earnings into your bank account.

Note: when you click on "Complete account setup," you will be shown a form that is already partially filled with the information you provided earlier. You need to make sure that all the information is correct. Then fill out the new required fields and submit the form. For instance, make sure you have provided the correct zip code, phone number, home address, etc.

We have been talking about setting up a Shopify store – before we end this chapter, let's talk briefly on other ways of creating a dropshipping store without using Shopify.

Shopify alternatives

After the 14 days trial period, Shopify charges you $29/month (for the basic plan) if you want to continue using the platform. Some people consider this expensive, especially new dropshippers. If you think Shopify is expensive, there are cheaper options you can explore.

WordPress and AliDropship

You can create a fully functional e-commerce website, just like the one you could create using Shopify. The process is similar to what you would do when creating a Shopify store. You need to create a WordPress site, install an e-commerce WordPress theme, and install the AliDropship plugin on your WordPress site.

The WordPress site with e-commerce theme installed will give you all the functionalities of an e-commerce website. The AliDropship plugin you will install will be used to import products from aliexpress.com directly into your store. We can say that AliDropship plug-in is to WordPress what Oberlo is to Shopify.

WordPress is a popular content management system that can be used to create, update, or manage a website. Just like Shopify, you can create an e-commerce store using WordPress by simply installing an e-commerce theme. Once you are done customizing the site, you will then install the AliDropship plug-in which will help you to import products directly to your store.

Using WordPress to create your e-commerce store will require that you will buy a domain name and a hosting package. Your domain could be the name of your store while your hosting package is for storing the contents of your website on the internet. An example of a domain name is www.janestores.com.

While many people prefer Shopify because it is a platform that is solely dedicated to the creation and management of e-commerce websites, and it actively supports dropshipping; the truth remains that Shopify is a bit expensive.

Apart from the monthly fees that Shopify charges you – you are also charged a certain transaction fee for every credit card transaction. Shopify's cheapest plan, which goes for $29 per month, still doesn't offer you all the options. The biggest package that Shopify offers goes for as high as $2,000/month. That's a lot of money for a new dropshipper to pay.

Creating your dropshipping website using WordPress and AliDropship might be a better option. You only need to pay for a domain name, a hosting package, and then AliDropship. Unlike Shopify's fees, you only pay for AliDropship once – no monthly fees. You could get a domain name for as low as $10 per annum and a hosting package for $12/month. So, when observed carefully, you see that going the WordPress/AliDropship option is cheaper.

Here are the steps you need to take to create a dropshipping store using WordPress (this is a quick summary):

1. Buy a hosting package
2. Buy a domain name
3. Download and install WordPress
4. Download and install an e-commerce WordPress theme
5. Customize your e-commerce website

6. Install AliDropship

7. Import products from aliexpress.com into your store and start selling.

The above is a quick summary of how you can create and manage a dropshipping store using WordPress and AliDropship. I did not want to do over the steps in detail because this is not a book on WordPress development. If you want to learn how to customize a WordPress website, then you might consider sourcing materials on that. Alternatively, you could outsource the customization of the site to a professional website developer.

In a subsequent chapter, we shall look at ways of marketing your products and driving traffic to your store.

Chapter Three:
Marketing your products

As a Shopify dropshipper, no one will see the products you have in your store unless you market them aggressively. If you must make sales, then get ready to go out there and let people know about the products you have in your store.

Now, there are several ways through which you can advertise your store and drive or generate traffic. In this section, we shall be looking at some of those ways. Typically, we have two main ways of driving traffic to a store – organic and paid traffic.

When you make posts on your social media timeline about the products you have in your store and leave a link to the store or product page, that's a good example of organic traffic. You are not paying for it. You can also get free or organic traffic when you create guests posts on blogs and include a link to your store in the call-to-action section.

One problem with free or organic traffic generation methods is that they take time to yield results and the result just trickle in like water. Unless you are a big social media influencer, relying on organic traffic sources should not be your best option. Rather, you should facilitate your results by paying for traffic.

One of the best traffic sources as far as dropshipping is concerned is Facebook PPC (pay per click advertising). What makes it great is that if you do it well, you will receive huge traffic in your store. Facebook ads as it is often called allows you to target people who are actively interested in the types of products you are selling.

It doesn't give you room to guess randomly – you can target people within a certain demographic; you can target people who live in a particular area. You can also target those who have purchased something online in the last few months or weeks.

Facebook collects the data of users on almost every other online platform – that's the data they use to improve their ads service. Another great feature of Facebook ads is that you are only charged when someone sees or clicks on the ad. It is not like some other ad methods where you are charged whether people see the ads or not.

If people don't get to see your ads, Facebook will not charge you – so, it is a win-win for you. Interestingly, running Facebook ads is cheap – with as little as $5, you can run high converting ads and send a lot of traffic to your store. When you compare the amount you will spend on the ads and the massive traffic you will get; then Facebook ads is worth it.

To run Facebook ads, here are the steps you should follow:

Note: creating high converting Facebook ads is a course on its own – and it is not something we can cover in this guide. If you desire to learn more about how to run effective ads, then consider getting some materials on the topic. What we shall present to you here are just the necessary steps.

Step 1: Create a Facebook page – you need a Facebook page to run Facebook ads. You cannot run ads using your personal Facebook account. When creating a page, make sure the name of the page represents the type of products you sell.

Step 2: Go to your page, and click on "Ad center," then "create ad." You will be required to give your campaign a name and state what you want to achieve with your ad. The options are there for you to choose from – do you want to increase exposure for your page? Do you want to send traffic to an external source like a website or e-commerce store? You will see many options you can choose from.

Step3: Select your target audience – you can set up your ad so that only people within a certain location will see them. You can also set up the ads so that only people who earn a certain income range will see the ads.

Step 4: Ad creative and ad copy – ad creative is the image or video that accompanies an ad. People prefer using videos as their ad creative – the logic is that videos convert better than images. You can also use images. Whatever you are using as your ad creative, make sure it relates with your product. In fact, if you are using an image, it should be a photo of the product you are advertising. It should be catchy enough to make the impatient Facebook user scrolling through their timeline to stop and look.

Your ad copy is the text that accompanies your ad image – you use it to explain what's in it for the viewer. If your ad text is not convincing enough or doesn't have a lot of incentives for the Facebook user, they would not bother to click on your ads.

A good way to learn how to write ad copies is to start observing some of the different Facebook ads that pop up occasionally on your Facebook timeline. Whenever you are scrolling through Facebook, watch out for ads and see how the advertisers crafted their copy and the type of creative they have used. This will help you to learn to craft your own ad copies and develop the best ad creative.

Step 5: Set your budget – Facebook allows you to set or determine how much you would like to spend running an ad every day. If you want to spend only $5, you can set it. Facebook will not charge you more than your daily budget.

Once you are done setting up and customizing the ad, publish the ad and wait for approval from the Facebook team. Normally, your ad will be reviewed to ensure that it meets all the standards. If you have followed the guidelines, then your ad should be approved without delay.

Once the ad has been approved, you can then sit back and watch the traffic that comes to your store. Create more ad campaigns using different ad sets and learn the one that performs better. This is called A/B split testing. When you have determined the ad sets that give you the best results, stick to it.

Remember, the steps above are just an overview – like mentioned earlier, learning how to run effective Facebook ads is a course on its own. You could consider getting some materials on the topic to broaden your knowledge. Also, as you continue to run ads, you will learn more about how to customize and optimize your ads for better results.

Other means of driving traffic to your store

Instagram influencers

Instagram has gradually moved from being a photo-sharing platform to a powerful marketing tool. Businesses have since learned that they could attract a lot of customers by simply posting about their business on Instagram.

What makes Instagram great is that it receives a lot of monthly visitors. At the moment, more than 800 million people visit the platform monthly. Do you know what that means? You will be exposing your business to many people.

Another thing that makes Instagram great is that many business owners are yet to see the hidden potentials of Instagram as a marketing tool. Many of these marketers still look at Instagram as a photo-sharing app that is only good for sharing vacation pictures. Other marketers are still digging it out on Facebook to care about Instagram marketing. However, if you should take your business to Instagram, you will be among the early birds who will leverage the platform to record huge sales.

There are three ways you could promote your store on Instagram:

- Build a huge audience
- Run Instagram ads – similar to Facebook ads
- Pay Instagram influencers to promote your products

To build a massive audience on Instagram takes time – you might need to spend months to achieve it. Also, you will need to be consistently posting useful content to retain your following. For the average dropshipper who just wants to send traffic to their store and make money, this might seem like a long process. The other options available to such a dropshipper is to run Instagram ads.

Even though growing an audience on Instagram takes time, and won't give you instant results, you still need to do it. This is how to go about it – while running Instagram ads or working with influencers, make sure you are also growing your own following at the same. By the time your audience has grown to a reasonable number, you could stop working with influencers and start posting marketing content directly on your page.

While you are waiting for your audience to grow, start with Instagram ads – the way to run it is just similar to the way you run Facebook ads. You decide your target audience, set up ad creative and copy, set your budget, and you are good to go. Instagram ads convert just like Facebook ads, if not better. When it is set up correctly, it can be a huge source of traffic to your store.

Apart from the two options above, you could work with an Instagram influencer to help you drive traffic to your store. Who is an Instagram influencer?

An Instagram influencer is just an Instagram user that has grown a large following through the relevant content they share on the platform. Influencers also record huge engagements on their posts – so, it is clear that if you pay them to market your product, you will get good results. Typically, anyone that has up to 50k followers could be considered an influencer. Although it depends on the industry – for some industries, people with 10k followers are considered influencers too.

Influencer marketing, which involves paying influencers to market a product started becoming popular the moment social media started taking center stage in the lives of many people. Today, influencer marketing is considered a viable way of marketing a product or service. It will also continue to be relevant in the coming years.

One thing that makes influencer marketing work well is that people who follow influencers see them as a hero and would be glad to do something that the influencer has asked them to do. Influencers are seen as people who are more knowledgeable on a subject, and when they recommend a product or service, their followers follow their recommendations.

To find an influencer in your niche, use the Instagram search feature. Search for users in your niche with a huge following. Observe their posting patterns and how many people engage with their posts. Go through their posts and observe if they have helped people to post sponsored content in the past. Send the influencer a direct message and let them know you would want to work with them.

When searching for an influencer, you have to be careful, so you don't pay money to someone with fake followers. How do you know someone with followers? It is simple – observe the number of their followers that engage with their posts and juxtapose it with the number of followers they have. If someone has 100k followers, for instance, and less than 100 people engage with their posts, it goes to show you that the majority of the followers are bot-generated.

You don't want to pay money to someone whose posts don't record a lot of engagement. Some dishonest people pay money to get bot-generated followers on Instagram – make sure you don't work with such people as that will amount to a waste of your resources.

If you have done your due diligence and chosen an influencer to work with, send them a direct message. Let them know you want them to give you a shoutout. Shoutout means a promotional post. Negotiate a price with the influencer and send them the image of the product you want to promote. The influencer will include a link to your store in their bio and ask their followers to click on the link to get the advertised product.

When working with an influencer, make sure the influencer does not make the promotional post sound so salesy. Rather, you would want them to craft the post in a way that would seem that they are only trying to recommend a product they have used before. Even without being told, good influencers know that they are supposed to make promotional posts seem like recommendations.

Depending on your agreement with the influencer, the shoutout post might remain on the page of the influencer for a day, week, month, or several months. The amount you will pay for the post to remain on an influencer's page for one day will differ from the amount you will pay for the post to be there for one month.

How much does an influencer charge? There is no fixed amount for influencer marketing. The amount you will pay will depend on so many factors such as your negotiating ability, the influencer involved, how many days you want the post to remain up, and even the type of product you are promoting. On average, the cost of influencer marketing will not dig a hole in your pocket, and the results can be quite encouraging. Many Shopify dropshippers use influencer marketing to drive traffic to their store.

Remember, when using influencer marketing, you need to be building your own audience at the same time. You might one day become an influencer and start marketing your products yourself and that of other people.

In this chapter, we have just talked about some of the popular ways of marketing your dropshipping business to attract huge sales. In the next chapter, you will learn about how to do product research.

Chapter Four:

Product research

Deciding to sell a product without, first of all, researching about the product to determine its viability can be likened to placing the cart before the horse. One of the things that differentiates a good dropshipper from the average one is that the former does a lot of research before selling a product while the latter just sells every product that comes to their mind.

Product research in dropshipping is like keyword research in blogging – it should be the first thing you do before deciding to sell a product. That being said, here are some of the top product research tools for a Shopify dropshipper:

1. salesource.io

This is a product research tool par excellence – it does so many things, some of which include:

- It helps you to know how many other stores are selling a particular product. Why is this information important? So you will know the number of stores you are competing with. If the competition is too stiff, you could consider leaving the product.

- The tool, even though it is mainly for product research, helps you to find good themes for your store. It also helps you to customize your listing by giving you product description suggestions.

- The tool compiles a list of products you could list in your store and start making sales immediately. The products span across more than 20 categories, so you are sure to find something that fits your niche.

- It has a Google Chrome browser extension which you can install to make it easier for you to use the tool.

As you can see, the product has many pros – the only perceived downside is that the tool provides you with a lot of information which could leave you confused and wondering the exact one to use.

2. nichescrapper.com

This great product research tool has both a free version and a paid version. The paid version costs about $13 per month – if you can afford the cost, the tool is totally worth having. As a beginner dropshipper, this tool is a must-have – it does provide you with a list of hot selling products which you can start selling immediately. The tool also has a Facebook ad generator, which you can use to create effective Facebook ads that convert.

The only downside is that since the tool provides you with a list of already researched products to sell, there will be many marketers selling the same product. Other than that, it is such a great tool.

3. ecomhunt.com

This product research tool is similar to the one mentioned above, with a slightly different user interface. The price of the tool is quite okay for all the useful information it provides you. The only downside is that it just shows you products that every other dropshipper is already selling.

4. productlistgenie.com

This product research tool is great for finding hot selling products that you can list on your store – some people have complained that it is a bit overpriced. It has a lot of cool features which include review generator, and it also integrates with Oberlo to help you find the best products. It provides you with a list of about 10k products which you can sell, especially if you don't want to start doing your own research from scratch.

5. Saturation inspector chrome extension

This is a Google Chrome extension – if you install it – anytime you are browsing the aliexpress.com website searching for a product, the tool lets you know if a product is saturated or not. This way, you don't have to import saturated products that everyone is selling into your store.

Here are you have it, some of the top product research tools for Shopify. Make sure you do product research before listing any product. Note: you can do your own research and come up with your own preferred product research tool.

Chapter Five:

Dropshipping suppliers

To work as a dropshipper, you need to find a fast-moving product and look for a supplier who will supply this product to your customers. The earliest form of dropshipping was done as a form of retail arbitrage. Sellers would typically look for cheaper products manually and sell the products at a higher cost.

In those days, the prevalent avenue for selling such products was social media – that was in the early days of social media. Although so many people still do retail arbitrage today, the number of those doing it has reduced significantly. It is safe to say that retail arbitrage gave way for dropshipping to take center stage.

Dropshipping became popular when people realized they could source for a cheaper product directly from manufacturers in China and ship same to Europe and America. Since labor is cheap in China, the cost of producing goods is also significantly cheaper than what you would get in the United States or Europe.

So, dropshippers took advantage of that to make a profit – even after adding shipping cost and production cost, the dropshippers found that they still made a profit. And that was how dropshipping grew to become a viable business model that we know it to be today.

Just like any other business, dropshippers soon discovered that there was a problem with their business model. It takes close to two weeks and sometimes three weeks for goods ordered from China to arrive in the United States or Europe successfully. This started to raise concerns because customers were beginning to get angry and raise eyebrows.

To solve the problem, dropshippers have resorted to sourcing products in the United States to deliver to a US audience. This is an advanced form of retail arbitrage or digitalized retail arbitrage because unlike the conventional person that does retail arbitrage, the dropshipper has developed means of using automation tools to source for cheaper products and sell the same on platforms where they are costlier.

The most popular platform where dropshippers source their products is Alibaba.com. This is a well-known Chinese e-commerce marketplace where customers could buy anything ranging from electronic gadgets to clothing items. One good thing about Alibaba.com is that the site displays in the English language, unlike other similar platforms where you would need to translate the language for you to understand it.

In addition to Alibaba.com, aliexpress.com is another good Chinese marketplace for sourcing products. In fact, aliexexpress is way more popular than Alibaba.com. The platform also has a lot of plug-ins or software tools that have been developed to help dropshippers source products from the platform and ship to different countries of the world. In the previous sections of this guide, we have looked at ways of dropshipping products from aliexpress.com to different locations.

As mentioned earlier, shipping products or goods from aliexpress.com to any part of the United States or Europe takes nothing less than two weeks. As a result, so many customers complained that shipments arrived late. Another problem was that some customers do get angry and cancel their order before the goods arrived, making the dropshipper to lose money.

To contain the problem, dropshippers started to source products directly from their location. This is referred to as local dropshipping in some quarters. So instead of heading to aliexpress.com or any of the other Chinese marketplaces to scout for products, dropshippers used automation tools to find products that are cheaper in one place and sell the same in another place.

The only problem with the above model is that the profit margins are way lower than what you would get had you shipped from China. Also, some of the local merchants from whom dropshippers get their products also frown at dropshipping as a business model. Although the number of merchants that are cool with dropshipping far outnumbers the number of those that don't vibe with the model.

We have talked about dropshipping from aliexpress.com extensively in a previous section of this book. For now, we want to talk about some of the suppliers within the United States who can help dropshippers deliver their products.

Dropshipping suppliers within the United States

As mentioned earlier, one of the benefits of using a dropshipping supplier that is based in the United States is that your customers will get to have their orders delivered in record time. Typically, it takes about three days or even a day for a supplier within the United States to deliver orders within the country.

Remember, we live in a world where people want everything to be instant. Imagine having your customer wait for close to two weeks before they get their orders delivered. Some customers will get angry and cancel their order with you. Some might even forget that they placed an order with a dropshipper. It happens all the time; you would get in touch with a customer to remind them that their order has arrived and you would hear things like, "I cannot remember placing such an order." In that case, you just have to count your losses or start using the product.

In the e-commerce business space, customer satisfaction is more important than any other thing. Customer satisfaction has to do with many things – it has to do with how the products you are selling is helping to meet the needs of the customer. It also has to do with the overall experience of the customer ordering a product from you. If you keep a customer waiting for more than two weeks, they might have negative things to say about your business and would never order from you again. So, you want to give the customer a positive experience.

That being said, here are some of the reasons why using a US-based supplier is preferred:

1. It offers fast shipping – the importance of fast shipping cannot be overemphasized. When customers order a product from you, they expect it to be delivered as soon as possible. Imagine

delivering a product to a customer the day after they made the order; it means you just got yourself a satisfied client. Remember, a satisfied client will turn to a repeat client, and in business, repeat customers are the lifeblood of the business.

It costs way less to keep an existing customer than to acquire a new one. For an existing customer, you have to say a few words to convince them to buy another product from you. However, for a potential customer, you will need to deploy so many marketing strategies becoming convincing them to buy from you. This is why it is often emphasized that you should prioritize the experience of your customers. Give them a positive experience and ones to remember. Once you do that, then expect them to keep buying from you.

Most United States based suppliers will deliver an order within a day or two, I have mentioned this severally. This is unlike what is obtainable when you are ordering from China where it could take up to 2 weeks or even a month in most cases for ordered products to get shipped to the destination.

2. Reliable tracking – most foreign-based suppliers make use of courier service companies that don't offer reliable tracking for shipped goods. When you use such suppliers, it is hard to track the progress of an order. You will not be able to pinpoint the exact location where your order has gotten to until it arrives at its destination. Sometimes, an order could get lost in transit – this is something that happens more often.

If you have ever ordered anything online, you will understand that online shoppers often want to know where their ordered product is at every point in time. They want to know the exact time they will get the product. They don't want to be kept in the dark as regards the location of the product they paid for. Many times, if the customer is unable to locate their product, they could get anxious, and some even decide to cancel their order.

Aliexpress.com, for instance, is just a marketplace, and like every other marketplace, different vendors create a storefront on the platform and market their goods. Now, when you order a product from an aiexpress.com supplier, they are going to try to reduce shipping costs. Most often, they go for the cheapest shipping options – some of those courier service providers used by the suppliers in China do not offer you a tracking code or anything of such with which you could track your order. Even some of them that give you a tracking code, you may find out that the data you get through the code could be incorrect.

On the contrary, when you use a local supplier, you are sure they are going to use a reliable tracking system to point you to the location of your order or product at every point in time. Most of the US suppliers use trusted courier service providers like DHL, FedEx, UPS, etc. to ship products. These courier service providers will offer you a tracking code which you can then forward to your clients. Your clients will use the tracking code to track their orders until it arrives at their destination successfully.

In addition to fast shipping, reliable tracking adds to the positive experience of the customer and would make them want to buy from you over and over again. Note: most customers don't want to be left in the dark – if you turn out to be the vendor who gives them the least anxiety, then you have gotten yourself some repeat clients. Remember what we said earlier about repeat customers – they are the best types of customers you would want to do business with.

3. You have a wider range of shipping options – US-based suppliers use better courier service providers, as mentioned earlier; as a result, they offer you a wide range of improved shipping options. For instance, you could choose that you want your customer's item to be delivered the same, the next day or within two days. Of course, if you choose

same-day delivery, you are going to pay a higher fee, but then, you will be giving your customers a better experience, and you could also transfer the cost to your customer.

This is not possible when you are sourcing suppliers from China or other overseas locations. For the most part, the product ordered will not arrive until after several days. So, if your customer needs their order urgently, you become handicapped. If many customers discover that you don't offer a shorter delivery time, they may be pushed to look elsewhere to get their needs.

The above are some of the shipping benefits of using a US-based supplier. The idea is that since the supplier is within the same location as the customer, the delivery time is greatly reduced and contributes to the overall experience of the customer. Do not forget that a happy customer will become a repeat customer.

Now, apart from the shipping benefits attached to using a US-based supplier, there are several other benefits that come with such practice. We shall get to talk about all of them one after the other.

Product benefits

There is no denying the fact that the product you get from US-based dropshipping suppliers will trump the ones you get from Chinese dropshipping suppliers in terms of quality. This is why such products are generally more expensive than the ones you get from China and other places.

For the most part, labor is way cheaper in China than the United States – this contributes to making the products gotten from there to be cheap. Also, there are not a lot of regulatory standards or guidelines – that's why many of the manufacturers in China tend to compromise on quality.

Now, to get United States-based dropshipping suppliers, you will be paying a higher amount of money for each product. But it is worth it – you will have the assurance that your customers are getting the best quality. Also, you will transfer the cost of the products to your customer – this is one of the joys of doing business, you will always transfer costs to the customer. Initially, your customer might protest about the price of your products, especially when there are several other dropshippers offering cheaper options. However, after attesting to the quality of the product you sell, they will have no other option than to stick with you.

To get your customers to patronize you, what you need to do is to convince them that your products are of higher quality than those that come in from Vietnam, Taiwan, China, or any of the other Asian countries where labor is relatively cheaper. As mentioned earlier, it just takes your customers knowing that they are paying for quality for them to patronize you.

Furthermore, if you source your products from the United States, they will have that "American-made" stamp of approval. There is no doubt that most patriotic people will prefer to buy a product made in the good old America than the ones that come from other sources. This is not saying that Americans wouldn't buy from other sources, but they will place a premium on their very own before considering other options.

If you are getting your products from United States-based dropshipping suppliers, most of the goods will be made in America and will carry that stamp of approval. This will help to distinguish you from the average dropshipper on eBay or Shopify who just orders supplies from outside sources.

Additionally, when your customers are assured that they are paying for a quality product that has met all the regulatory standards or guidelines, they will be more likely to buy at higher retail prices. You just need to know how to state it that your products are from the US and your customers will be more than happy to pay a higher price for it.

Yes, there will be those who will prefer the cheaper alternatives from China and other Asian countries, but the vast majority of customers who understand what it means to pay for quality products will happily pull out their wallet and pay you the right monetary worth of the product you are selling.

Apart from the above benefits of using US-based dropshipping suppliers, there are several others. For instance, it helps you to give your customers better satisfaction and experience. Imagine delivering the orders of your customers to them within a day, something that takes other vendors days or weeks to do, what do think would be the experience of that customer? Of course, they are going to speak good things about you and your business.

Imagine making sure that the customer gets a comprehensive tracking system that lets them know the exact location of their ordered product at every point in point. Again, what do you think will be the experience of the customer? Their experience will be positive, and you will reap the benefits in that you will acquire a repeat customer for yourself.

The benefits of using a US-based dropshipping supplier are just too enormous. We have not mentioned that it is a perfect way to distinguish yourself among the crowd. The majority of dropshippers are still using Chinese based dropshipping suppliers to fulfill an order. This makes it really hard for such dropshippers to give their customers a better experience all the time. If you join only a few dropshippers who use local dropshipping suppliers, it means you will make more sales, since there are not a lot of people doing that. How will you make more sales?

Simple – once you explain to your customers who are mostly based in the United States, Canada, Europe, etc. that they will get expedited shipping, then you have already won yourself a customer. Some customers might protest the higher cost of the products you are selling as opposed to what is available in other places. You could calm their mind or neutralize their fears by letting them know that they are getting better quality.

This is not to mention that the "Made in USA" stamp that your products will carry will further improve your credibility and make more customers want to order from you. While some customers may not really care about where their ordered supplies are coming from, many others do care, and once they are sure that the products are made locally, they will pay you the money you have quoted for the products.

In order not to romanticize things a lot, it is good that I mention that many US dropshipping suppliers charge considerably higher than their foreign-based counterparts – there are some customers who still prefer the cheaper options. For some of them, they often don't tend to understand why they should pay a higher amount for a product that they could get cheaper elsewhere.

If you are a focused business owner, you should be able to know how to make your business distinct and know who your customers are. If you have determined that your audience are those who can willingly pay a higher price for quality, then stick with them and forget about the customers that prefer cheaper options. In business, it is called knowing your audience or market segment and sticking with them.

What to consider before choosing a US dropshipping supplier

Remember, as a dropshipper, you are a business owner, and as a business owner, you need to think critically and strategically. No matter the type of dropshipping supplier you want to use, it is still necessary that you do your due diligence before pitching your tent with anyone. You do not want to work with a supplier solely based on the fact they are based in the United States. That will be a really infantile reason to work with someone. On the other hand, you don't want to work with a supplier solely based on the fact that they are based in China, Vietnam, or other overseas locations.

Also, you don't want to work with a supplier on a first name and handshake basis. Remember, as a dropshipper, your supplier is one of your most critical business partners. If they mess up or if you choose the wrong one, then your business suffers. In fact, it is safe to say that you are at the mercy of your supplier. If they decide to mess you up and continually send wrong packages to your customers, then your business will be as good as gone. If the supplier sends damaged products to your customer, you will get nothing but negative reviews, ratings, and feedback – which will impact you negatively.

There are just so many ways through which your supplier could ruin your business – and that's why you must properly vet any supplier before settling for them. One thing I normally tell people who want to go into dropshipping for the first time – find and join forums or communities of other dropshippers. In those forums, you can ask questions about suppliers and get the most honest answers from people who have had firsthand experience with the suppliers in question.

There are several active dropshipping groups both on Facebook, Reddict.com, and other online mediums. You just need to search, find, and join as many forums as possible. When you join, make sure you contribute to discussions – that way, when you ask questions, other members of the community will be more willing to answer you.

That being said, here are some of the things you should consider when choosing a US-based dropshipping supplier:

1. Trust and reliability

The best way to know the reliability of a supplier you want to pitch your tent with is to ask for recommendations If you are a member of a community of dropshippers, there is a chance that other dropshippers have used the supplier you are asking about. You can ask the supplier for references – let them refer you to some of the dropshippers they have worked with – this is a good way of sieving out the unreliable ones.

Additionally, you could check websites like TrustPilot.com to read what other people are saying about the supplier. Do note that some suppliers or companies do pay individuals to leave positive reviews about their business on TrustPilot. So, if you want to depend on what you see on the platform, make sure you ignore the shiny positive 5-star reviews.

If you really want to get an honest opinion about the supplier and any other company at all on TrustPilot, look out for the 2 and 3-star reviews. Those are the real unbiased opinions of people who have used the services of the company. You could also check the 1-star reviews, but in most cases, it has been discovered that some of the people who leave such reviews are disgruntled elements who just want to pull down other people's business.

You can also go through this webpage that provides you a list of more than 8,000 vetted dropshipping suppliers you could work with. This is not expressly saying you should just pick one or more suppliers from the list and work with them without doing your own due diligence. Of course, you will still need to ask other dropshippers about the suppliers you want to work with – this is to help get the opinions of others.

If you want to take things, you could arrange to meet the supplier face to face and talk over things with them over a cup of coffee. Although this is a stressful option, the result will be worth it. At least, you get to know who you are working with as well as know who to hold accountable if anything goes wrong.

2. Friendliness and communication

What is the ease of doing business with the supplier you want to choose? Are they friendly? Can they work with you to resolve issues should there be any? Will they cooperate with you and ensure that your customers get a good experience or do they suddenly go cold once you have paid them? Yes, there are some suppliers that will display a totally different before you have made payment and then turn around to cold uncooperative, difficult fellows once they have gotten your money. Working with such suppliers will dent your business because they may refuse to provide tracking codes or when they might provide the codes late, making your customer be anxious.

Remember, when working with a supplier, you would want to partner with them for a long time. The reason is that you want to be going through the hassle and vetting and choosing a new supplier every other week. This means you should do your best to choose someone you can easily get on with. Again, it is important to ask other dropshippers their experience with a supplier you want to work with. When asking, don't just focus on the reliability of the supplier, ask about how friendly they are and how they treat dropshippers that work with.

Even without asking others, if you are discerning enough, you could tell a lot about the character or personality of a person through their emails or voice. If they exude some irrational nastiness when you are still talking or negotiating with them, then there is a high chance they will exhibit their full unruly attitude when you have committed you and/or your client's money into their care. Once you have ascertained that the supplier you want to work with is friendly and approachable, then go on to check how much they charge for shipping products.

3. Shipping costs and information

You opted for a US--based dropshipping supplier because you wanted your customers to receive their orders as soon as possible. Now, would it make sense to choose a supplier that delays delivery? If a US-based supplier cannot facilitate fast shipping, then there is no difference between them and the one based in China, for instance.

Before choosing a US-based supplier, ensure you know about all the shipping options they offer. Do they offer same-day shipping? Next day shipping, etc.? You would want to know. In addition, you will need to know about their shipping costs. By knowing the shipping costs for each item beforehand, you will know how to charge your customers for products ordered properly.

4. Production capacity

Some dropshipping suppliers are also the manufacturers of the products they supply. If you want to partner with such a supplier, you need to ask them about their production capacity. This will give you an idea of how many products they can make at a time. Why is this important? You don't want to run into a situation in the future where you will have to start sourcing for another supplier when your main supplier has run out of stock.

During the holiday seasons, a lot of people are often shopping for supplies, if you partner with a supplier that doesn't have enough production capacity, the frustration that comes with not finding what one wants could drive your customers away. If a supplier is able to meet up with your demands, it means you will never have to put up that "out of stock" label that many customers hate to see.

5. Additional fees

So many suppliers charge what they call a dropshipping fee – this is normal and you should expect it. However, the supplier has to be upfront with you about these fees – you don't want to be greeted with surprises when you have already ordered for some supplies. Additionally, you need to know what the price you are being charged covers.

Some suppliers will remove every branding symbol that has to do with them. Some others will package the product in your preferred packing style or box. Some of them will also issue an invoice in your business name to the customer. These are some of the things that the dropshipping fees cover, but you should not just assume, ask first.

If a supplier cannot state what they plan to do with the fees they want to charge you, then you are better off looking elsewhere. Also, if they charge inordinate fees that cannot be justified, you should look elsewhere too. You are in business to make profits – if you have to lose all your profits through random fees, then how are you going to make a profit?

6. Warranty and returns

As a dropshipper, your customers are humans, and as humans, they could change their mind after ordering a product and then decide to return it. If such happens, what will your supplier do? Will take part of the responsibility or will they shift all the responsibility over to you? Remember, when you pay dropshipping fees to a supplier, these are some of the things they are supposed to protect you against.

So, before you choose a supplier, make sure you read their returns policy. They should also provide you with information about product guarantee and warranty. What happens in the event that a customer receives a damaged product? Who bears the cost? This is a sensitive area in dropshipping because most suppliers like to absolve themselves of any form of blame or responsibility when an issue arises.

If a supplier sends the wrong product to your customer, will they bear the risk of reshipping the right product to the same supplier? Or will they require you to pay more money? If a customer decides that they are not happy with their order, will the dropshipping supplier gladly receive the product back without a fuse?

Sometimes, you have to go beyond what the supplier says concerning their return policy. Most of the time, some suppliers say things they do not put into practice. To get the best opinion about the return policies of a supplier of interest, you are better off getting the views of other dropshippers who might have used the supplier. Nothing beats the firsthand opinions of real dropshipper in issues like this, so don't take it for granted.

Note: depending on the different types of products you are selling, you will need more than one supplier. Even if you are selling only one item, you may still need more than one supplier depending on the location of your customer. Some suppliers are better suited for customers based in a particular area than the others. So, no matter the number of suppliers you need, make sure you put the points mentioned above into consideration before settling for anyone.

Now that we have covered the top six things you should consider when choosing a dropshipping supplier in the United States, here are the top ten dropshipping suppliers in the United States.

1. iFuncity (mostly supplies electronics like cameras and photography equipment)

Since its inception in 2007, iFuncity has been a dropshipping supplier of choice in the United States. The company has served more dropshippers in more than 60 countries, and partnering with them for the supply of electronic gadgets will not be a wrong choice.

One thing that makes the company stand out is that they offer what is called blind dropshipping service. What is blind dropshipping? If a company offers blind dropshipping, it means that they customize the products and brand it with a dropshipper's branding material or after the taste of the dropshipper.

For instance, if your brand name is, "Grupo," and you want to order digital cameras from iFuncity, the company can brand the cameras to bear your business name and carry your logo. Also, the invoice will carry your brand name and every other information you want. This way, your customer will not know that the product was drop shipped. Blind dropshipping is also great because it helps to build your own brand and name.

In addition to offering in-demand electronics, the company also offers fashion accessories. The company gives you an option to choose between branded items and non-branded ones. So, if you want to brand your products before shipping, you indicate. On the other hand, if you want them to ship without branding, you can also state it.

If you want the company to be your dropshipping supplier, you can browse through their product inventory – you can also request for a product data feed, and the company will provide.

2. Teledynamics (mainly supplies computers and electronics)

Teledynamics is based in Austin USA, and they are mostly into the wholesale supply of electronics. They are one of the major distributors of electronics from manufacturers such as Polycom, Siemens, Motorola, Sony, SBC, AT&T, NEC, Panasonic, Plantronics and a host of others.

One good thing about the company is that they do require that you must order a certain quantity or what is called minimum order quantity (MOQ). And that's why they are a great option for dropshippers. Another exciting thing about the company is that, just like iFuncity, they also offer bling dropshipping and this they do at no extra cost.

To get started with Teledynamics, you will need to obtain reseller identification. To find products from the company to resell or dropship, simply request for the company product catalog. The companies generally prefer working with individuals with good credit rating.

3. FootwearUS

If you want to be dropshipping footwears, then this particular company is your best bet. One unique thing about the family-owned company is that they manufacture their footwear. Just the two other companies mentioned above, FootwearsUS offers blind dropshipping – if you want them to brand the wears with your name, just let them know and they will do it.

4. FragranceNet

This company has been in existence since 2007, and the name suggests, they are majorly into the supply of perfumes and colognes. To drop ship the company's products, you will need to sign up on their website as a dropshipper. Once you have signed up for the dropshipping program, then you will have access to all of the company's products.

If your customers are within the US, the company will charge you approximately $6 to ship each item. You will need to factor this shipping cost when giving your customers the retail prices of the products you sell. The amount the company will charge for shipping a product overseas will depend on the weight of the item and other factors.

5. I&I Sports Supply Company

This is a major supplier of airsoft products, martial arts merchandise, arcades, paintball products, etc. in the US. Like most of the other companies we have mentioned, this one also offers blind dropshipping.

6. Whitney Brothers

This is another great dropshipping supplier – the company is mainly into the supply of baby gear including children's furniture – great for daycare centers, nurseries, playrooms, etc. they offer a lifetime warranty for all their products.

7. New Concepts Distributors International

This dropshipping supplier is majorly into the distribution of underwear, shapewear, and other related clothing items. The company adds a nominal fee of $3.00 to all drop shipped products. So, if you want the company to drop ship products to your customers, they will add $3.00 to the price of the product – which is fair enough. The company doesn't have a minimum order quantity so they can happily ship a single item to your customer.

8. Innovative beauty

Just as the name of the company implies, they are mainly into the supply of beauty products – quality ones at reasonable prices. They have a special price for drop shipped items which will be made available to you upon request.

9. Fashion stories

This company offers drop shipping services for pieces of jewelry and other fashion accessories. The good thing about them is that they don't have a minimum order quantity – so they can happily ship even a single item to your customer.

10. Parkflyers RC

They are into the distribution of remote control toys. They offer blind dropshipping – if you want to join their dropshipping program, you will pay a one-time fee of $99 after which you will not pay any other extra fee per order.

Now, we have talked about some of the dropshipping suppliers in the US – you could be asking, "What can I do with such information?" Since most people who use Shopify to create their dropshipping store normally source their products directly from aliexpress.com suppliers, what can one do with US-based suppliers?

Let's face it, while drop shipping products from China is still largely popular, if you want to build a brand, one that will be attached to your name for a longer time, you need to start thinking strategically. How do you think strategically? Ask yourself, "Will dropshipping products from aliexpress.com make me known?"

The answer is no – you will make money, but you still do not have a brand. The ultimate winner in this whole game is still the aliexpress.com supplier and perhaps, Shopify. You might ask, "Why are the suppliers the winners?" Shopify is well known all over the world – whenever you mention Shopify, people already know that it is a platform for building dropshipping stores. In the same vein, if you mention aliexpress.com, people see the platform as a popular e-commerce marketplace. But when your brand or business name is mentioned, would anyone know you? The answer is no.

When you are just getting started as a dropshipper, it is good for you to use Shopify to make quick money, then start thinking of how to build your own brand. By building your brand, it doesn't mean you should start producing your own product. Rather, you should start branding the products you sell. You can still be a dropshipper, but you will no longer be the type that just dropships products from China to a customer.

The type of dropshipping that anyone should aspire to become is the type where you source products directly from the types of suppliers mentioned above, then list the products on your e-commerce website. When an order is placed, you send the details over to your supplier for them to fulfill the order. You could ask, "How is this different from the typical dropshipping?"

The difference between the model I have described above and the popular one is that you are using suppliers who offer blind dropshipping. The supplier will brand the product with your business name before shipping to your customers. The supplier will also make sure that the invoice sent to the customer carries your name or business name instead of that of the supplier.

By making sure that the products you dropship are branded with your name, it will really be easy for you to grow your assumed small dropshipping business into a global brand in no distant time. When your brand has grown quite huge, you could go into direct production of your own products and start charging as much as you want.

Like I have been reiterating all along, the problem with most dropshippers is that they don't see dropshipping as a long term business. For some people, dropshipping is just an avenue to raise quick cash or something they fall back on when they have lost their job or when they want to make some money for rent.

For such people who see dropshipping as a "hustle" rather than a business, they will often be trying to grab as much quick money as possible. Don't be like the others who see drop shipping as an interim hustle – instead, you should see dropshipping as a business that can launch you into global prominence.

If you want to work directly with a local supplier, you could do so with your Shopify store or a

WordPress store. The process is basically the same – instead of importing products from aliexpress and the other popular platforms, you simply do manual product listing. When an order is placed, you take the order details and send over to your supplier.

By the time you have developed a good working relationship with some supplier, you could arrange or negotiate better deals with them. For instance, you could tell them that for you to keep working with them, they should offer you reduced prices. A considerate dropshipping supplier will be happy to keep you and honor your reasonable demands.

Another significant advantage of this approach of dropshipping is that you are mostly in charge of your business. If Shopify, aliexpress.com or any of the others decide to restrict your operations or do something in that line, you could simply design your own e-commerce platform and work with your trusted suppliers to fulfill your orders.

Before we end this chapter, let's have a recap of all we have seen in the section so far.

We started the chapter by stating that dropshipping as a business model has come to stay and will continue to remain relevant as long as individuals are willing to stay in the comfort of their bedroom and have their products delivered to them.

The first set of dropshippers were basically doing retail arbitrage, then graduated into sourcing cheaper products from China and selling the same in the US and Europe. We identified that one of the problems associated with such a dropshipping model is that customers have to wait for up to two weeks to have their orders delivered. Another problem is that customers have to deal with inferior or low-quality products.

We were able to establish that the best way to contain the problem is to work with US-based or local dropshipping suppliers. These types of dropshipping suppliers mostly offer blind dropshipping service – they can brand your products with your business name or brand name before shipping them to your customers.

The choice of using local dropshipping suppliers is a better one as you are sure of the products you are getting and your customers get to have their orders delivered in record time. Working with a local supplier who offers blind dropshipping service also helps you to develop and build your own brand so that you don't spend all your years working to help other people's business or brand grow at the detriment of yours.

In the next chapter, we shall look at the possibility of dropshipping on Amazon.

Chapter Six:

Amazon dropshipping

When most people hear of dropshipping, the first thought that comes to their mind is Shopify. The reason for that is not hard to guess – Shopify has become a household name in the dropshipping industry and is the first name that comes to mind when dropshipping is mentioned.

Little do people know that they can also build their own dropshipping store or a general e-commerce store using WordPress and some plug-ins. Many others do not also know that they could dropship on eBay – yes, eBay actively supports dropshipping, but you have to play by their rules. Another platform which supports dropshipping, albeit surprisingly is Amazon.

Amazon allows dropshipping, but you must read and abide by their dropshipping policy. Some of the information contained in their dropshipping policy, which can also be found on their website include the following:

- You must identify yourself as the record seller of the products you dropship. What this means is that Amazon doesn't want a situation where a customer buys something from a supposed seller, and another supplier with a totally different name supplies the product.

- You must remove every label, invoice, marketing material, etc. that indicate that the products you are selling are coming from a third party. For instance, if you are using iFuncity as your supplier, the invoice of the product must not bear iFuncity. The packaging of the product should not have anything that links it with iFuncity. Basically, Amazon wants your supplier to offer you blind dropshipping services. Some of the suppliers we mentioned in the previous section do offer blind dropshipping; you can work with them and drop ship their products on Amazon.

- If a customer seeks to return a product, the seller, which in this case, is you must be the one to process the return and offer every needed assistance to the customer. Amazon does not want you to refer a customer to the supplier that drop shipped the product. To amazon, the customer does not know the dropshipping supplier; you and Amazon are the only parties known to the customer, so you must be available to process all returns.

- You cannot order products from another online retailer and have the retailer drop ship the product directly to a customer. By that, you are already prohibited from sourcing products from aliexppress.com or any of the other popular online retailers. You are then left with the option of ordering from local suppliers.

- You must be able to comply with all other Amazon policies regarding selling on the platform.

Apart from complying with the above rules, Amazon also expects you to drop ship using their FBA program. FBA simply means Fulfilment by Amazon – it is a program developed by Amazon where the company fulfills your orders on your behalf. When fulfilling the order, Amazon indicates that this product is sold by XYZ seller and fulfilled by amazon. The product also arrives at the customer's destination in Amazon packaging.

Amazon has what they call fulfillment centers that are scattered all over the country. When you join the FBA program, you will ship your products to any of the fulfillment centers, then when you get an order, Amazon ships the product on your behalf, Amazon also does customer support and everything in between for you. Then they will take a certain percentage of the price of the product and pay the remaining to you.

Amazon expects that you should dropship using their FBA program – this basically means you will get products from your suppliers and keep them in Amazon's fulfillment centers. When you get an order, Amazon helps you to ship the product to your customer. One problem with that arrangement is that your supplier might not agree to release their products to you without an initial or down payment. Also, you may have your reservations about making down payments for a product that no one has indicated interest in buying.

Normally, if you own your product, either through white labeling, or you manufacture the products yourself, then dropshipping using the Amazon FBA program can be a great option. However, when you are using a third-party supplier, joining the FBA program might not be the best option for you.

Amazon will start charging you what they call long term storage fees if your products stay in their fulfillment centers for more than six months without getting sold. As a dropshipper, you cannot afford to pay money to keep a product that people may not be interested in buying. The FBA program also has many other fees that may eat deep into your profit. Amazon has what they call FBA calculator, which you can use to calculate all the fees you will have to pay for dropshipping a particular product using the FBA program.

Since the FBA program is a total NO for a dropshipper, are there still ways of leveraging Amazon to make sales as a dropshipper? The answer is YES. However, you will have to be the one fulfilling your orders – Amazon calls it fulfillment by merchant.

Typically, you will create a seller account on Amazon, list some products, when you get an order, you send the order details to your supplier who drop ships the product in your branded package. Once your supplier has shipped the product, they will provide you with a tracking number which you can then supply to your customer for them to monitor the movement or status of their orders.

Advantages of dropshipping on Amazon

Dropshipping on Amazon has a lot of benefits that are too numerous to mention, but we are still going to talk about some of them.

One of the significant benefits is that you will be selling products on a platform that records millions of human traffic every day. Amazon currently has close to 30 million active users – this means you will be selling to this vast number of an active audience.

With such a huge user base, if you know how to position yourself before them, then you are sure to make money. Also, though the competition is high, you can still grab your own cut from the huge pie. Even if you are just able to convince only 0.001% of that audience to patronize you, that means you will still be smiling home at the end of every day.

Another major advantage of selling on Amazon is that the marketplace is already well known – you will enjoy what is called associative branding. By virtue of being on the platform, many customers will trust you enough to patronize your profits. Amazon has worked well over the years to perfect its branding – it is perceived as a company that places a premium on the interest of the customer. It is also seen as a company that wants to give every customer a positive experience. This is something that many customers are aware of, no wonder they like to patronize the huge marketplace. As said earlier, selling on Amazon will make you enjoy associative branding.

Unlike dropshipping on other platforms where you have to work really hard to convince the customer to trust you, Amazon's solid image will serve as an umbrella that covers you. Now, you can leverage this positive brand image and the massive traffic that comes to Amazon to make money. All you need is to position your products in a way that they are discovering on the platform. You can do that by ensuring you follow SEO best practices when listing your products.

The majority of buyers who come to Amazon do not bother to visit the different sections of the website when searching for a product. What they simply do is that they type the product they want into the search bar and follow the search results. Most of them don't even type the full name of the product; they just enter a few keywords that are associated with the product, then follow the search results to find the products they want.

Now, if you want such a customer to discover your product and buy them, then you have to think like them. See yourself as a potential buyer who has come on Amazon to buy your own product. What are the keywords you would type into the search box to be able to find your products? Think about those keywords and use them intuitively when listing your product. Include the keywords in the title and description of your product – that's the way that customers will find the product and buy it when they are doing searches.

What I have just described is called search engine optimization (SEO) – you are optimizing your listing and loading it with relevant keywords so that when potential buyers search for the type of products you sell, yours will pop up in the search results. One thing about Amazon is that if you master SEO and how to do it well, you will be making consistent sales on Amazon.

If you know how to do SEO on Amazon, then you may not need to pay money to advertise the products you sell. This is yet another huge advantage that is attached to selling on the Amazon platform. As mentioned earlier, Amazon has up to 30 million active users – with such a vast user base, you don't need to pull external traffic to your listing. All you need is to position your listing before the already present traffic and watch the magic that will happen.

Yes, you may wish to advertise your products using the Amazon PPC (pay per click) ad method, but it is not entirely necessary. In fact, if you have many products that are selling on the platform, and you know how to craft the best product descriptions, then you may not pay Amazon to run ads for your products. By saving the money you would have spent on running ads, you will actually have more money in your pocket.

Cons

Yes, dropshipping on Amazon does have its own drawbacks – it is like displaying your products in an open market where there are thousands, if not millions of other vendors like you who are also selling the same products. As expected, there will be stiff competition in such a marketplace.

Amazon is a vast marketplace, and many vendors have storefronts on the platform – no matter the type of products you would want to sell, there will be many other vendors who will be selling the same product. So, you will need to position yourself to make potential customers choose you instead of your competitors.

Many sellers set the prices of their products to be ridiculously low – it is their own strategy or way of beating the stiff competition. Most of them are usually dropshippers who order from an online retailer, who then ships directly to the customer – something that Amazon clearly frowns on but people do it anyway.

For such people, they don't really care about following set down rules; they are only happy when they make a profit no matter how little, even if it is just $1 on a profit. When vendors resort to making their products dirt cheap in order to beat the competition, how do you survive or compete with such people? That's one of the disadvantages of dropshipping on Amazon. Even though the competition is stifling, if you use a combination of good SEO practices combined with other factors such as good rating/feedback, then you can survive the competition.

Another major disadvantage is that you cannot order from another online retailer, who will then ship the product directly to the customer. This means you cannot order from an aliexpress.com supplier and have them ship the product to your customer, something you can do when using Shopify. It is one of the don'ts that Amazon included in their dropshipping policy.

Even though some people see that as a con, you can actually look at the bright side of things and see the policy as an advantage. At least, you will get to work with local suppliers, who will brand products using your name or brand name and then ship to your customers. Something that will help you grow a huge brand in the long run.

Another disadvantage, although some people may not really see it as a disadvantage, is that many Amazon customers have very high expectations. Once there is a little mistake, they would leave scathing feedback on your product, which would scare away other potential buyers. And if more people continue to leave such feedback, Amazon could close your account or withdraw your seller privileges.

Lastly, Amazon could wake up one morning and decide to restrict your account – as I always say, if another company can delete your business, then you don't really have a business. Yes, no business is immune from external influences, but the greater control of your business should be in your hands.

That being said, when you consider the cons and pros, you will see that dropshipping on Amazon is still worth it. Now, if you want to get started, here are a few steps you should take.

Getting started

Step 1: Decide on the type of products you want to sell

Amazon has more than 20 product categories and ten more are available to sellers with a professional account. Before proceeding to create an account, you need to decide on the type of product you would want to sell on the platform. Your choice has to be as unique as possible – you don't want to start selling the same product that millions of other sellers are also selling.

One common mistake that most dropshippers often make is that they go on the internet and search for "best products to sell on Amazon," then they just dive in and start selling the products they found in their search. One problem with selling the same products that one website described as hot-selling is that you are not the only person searching for such products.

The same way you are searching the internet for hot selling products, thousands of other dropshippers are also searching for such a product. All the people searching for such products will end up flooding the Amazon marketplace with the same product and then start complaining of low sales.

Think outside the box – don't go to the internet searching for a hot selling product. Instead, use your intuition and think about the products that you feel people really need. While brainstorming, you might just get product ideas that will change your story. Now, once you have determined the types of products you want to sell – the next thing you want to do is to negotiate with a supplier who will drop ship the products to your customers. Consider some of the dropshipping suppliers we mentioned in the previous section.

Remember, Amazon does not allow you to use online retailers to fulfill your orders – so, don't expect to use a marketplace like aliexpress.com to fulfill your orders. Even though many sellers do it, you don't want to be among them. If found to be using online retailers to fulfill orders, Amazon could suspend your account and make sure you don't receive the money you have earned.

Step 2: Register and choose a selling account

After deciding on the type of products you want to sell, the next step is to register an account on Amazon as a seller and choose your preferred selling plan. To register an account, click here, then click on "Start selling" to start the registration process. You will need to enter your email and name, as shown in the image below. Choose your password and proceed to the second stage of the registration.

amazon seller central

Create account

Your name

[   ]

Email

[   ]

Password

[At least 6 characters   ]

ⁱ Passwords must be at least 6 characters.

Re-enter password

[   ]

[Next]

Already have an account? Next ›

Once you have created your account, you will need to choose your selling plan. Amazon offers two selling plans – individual seller and professional seller. If you intend to list 40 products or less, then you have to go for an individual seller account. With an individual seller account, Amazon will charge you $0.99 for every sale you record.

The professional seller account offers you more flexibility in terms of the number of products you can sell. Unlike the individual seller account that allows you to list only 40 products, with a professional seller account, you can list an unlimited number of products. You can list as much as 10,000 products – that's if you will be able to fulfill all the orders that you will be getting.

Additionally, a professional seller account has a monthly fee of $39.99 every month. Once you have paid the fee, you will not have to pay $0.99 for every product sold, unlike what is obtainable with an individual seller account.

Step 3: List products

After creating a seller account and getting it approved, the next step is to list products and start selling. If you are using an individual seller account, you will only be able to list products individually. However, with a professional seller account, you can list or upload products in batches with the help of third party services or tools.

Step 4: Start selling

If the products you have listed are truly ones that people desire, you will start receiving orders in no time. Remember, Amazon is a huge platform with lots of available users – so if the products you have listed are truly relevant and needed, then you should expect to get your first order on the same day you listed your products. This is one of the reasons why you need to do proper research and ensure that you are not just selling the same product as thousands of other dropshippers.

Step 5: Fulfil your orders

Earlier, we mentioned that the FBA program is not the best for a dropshipper – you should go for FBM

(Fulfillment by Merchant). Once you receive an order, send the order details to your supplier – remind them that you prefer blind dropshipping. The supplier should not include their marketing material in the packaging of the product, and they should remove everything or material that will link them to the product. You want the product to have your brand name as the shipper.

If your customer confirms that they have received their order, the money for the product will be added to your Amazon balance, which will be paid to you at regular intervals. When you receive a payment, Amazon will send you a payment notification. Payments are usually sent directly to your bank account, which you must have provided during registration.

The above are the steps you need to follow to dropship on Amazon. Next, let's talk about another form of dropshipping – which involves dropshipping from Amazon to eBay.

Dropshipping from Amazon to eBay

This type of dropshipping is one that many dropshippers engage in – they find cheaper products on Amazon and sell them on eBay. Amazon is known for selling items at low prices – so dropshippers leverage that to make money on eBay. When the product is ordered on eBay, the dropshipper orders the same product on Amazon and ships to the customer. The profit the dropshipper makes is the difference between the price of the product on Amazon and the price the dropshipper listed it on eBay.

The above model cannot be said to be strictly dropshipping – retail arbitrage will be a more suitable term for it. The retailer scouts through the Amazon website looking for cheap deals, when they have found it, they list same on eBay and make a profit.

Now, there are a lot of problems with this model of dropshipping – one; the product usually gets to the buyer in Amazon packaging. If the customer discovers that their product arrived from Amazon instead of eBay, they could get angry. Also, the customer could find out that they could have gotten the product cheaper on Amazon rather than buying it from eBay. All this will contribute to a negative customer experience, which could make the customer leave negative feedback or even escalate the issue with eBay. In cases like that, eBay could suspend the account of the dropshipper.

Furthermore, if the Amazon seller that has the product discovers they have been used to drop ship their own product, they could get angry and take drastic actions. This was exactly what happened sometime in the past when an Amazon seller discovered that someone on eBay was selling his exclusive product at a far higher price. The Amazon seller went on eBay and purchased the product, then went on his product page on Amazon and increased the price of the product.

If the eBay seller fulfills the order, he will incur a huge loss – so, he canceled the order. The Amazon seller proceeded to leave a scathing review on the eBay seller's page, which affected him greatly. While eBay is not against dropshipping, the platform does not allow sellers to drop ship products from Amazon to eBay.

Apart from the argument that it is ethically wrong, eBay thinks that since customers will receive their orders in Amazon packaging, dropshipping from Amazon to eBay would mean helping Amazon grow their brand. Do not forget, Amazon and eBay are operating in the same market, so they are competitors, and no business would want to promote their competitors at their own detriment.

Other dropshipping options

Apart from dropshipping using your own e-commerce store, Shopify, Amazon or dropshipping from Amazon to eBay, you can dropship products from aliexpress.com suppliers or other suppliers to eBay. Yes, eBay fully supports dropshipping from other suppliers. What they don't support is dropshipping from Amazon to eBay. Recently, they have been restricting the privileges of accounts they suspect are dropshipping from Amazon to eBay.

To drop ship on eBay, you must be ready to abide by the rules – one of the rules states you must guarantee that customers will get their orders in less than 30 days. And as stated earlier, you should not drop ship from Amazon to eBay, although you can get your products from other suppliers. In fact, eBay states it clearly that you are not under any obligation to state that your products are coming from other suppliers – this means they support dropshipping fully.

In all of these, creating your own independent dropshipping store is still the best option although you will have to drive traffic to the store by yourself. You won't enjoy the huge traffic that comes to the big marketplaces. You won't also leverage associative branding to sell more. But it gives you control and flexibility.

Conclusion

Dropshipping has become popular within the last couple of years and will remain relevant in the coming years. The reason is simple – as more and more people gain access to the internet and mobile devices, they would want to order products online – which means more business for dropshippers.

There is no better time than now to join into the dropshipping bus – it is still largely profitable. You only need to do proper product research and be sure that you are not just doing what everyone is doing.

Also, if you want dropshipping to pay you well, you must take it as a business and have long term plans for it. If you see it as a side "hustle" that you run to when you are out of a job, then it will pay you like a side hustle.

Lastly, while drop shipping using Shopify, think about building your own independent e-commerce store. Then work with local suppliers to supply your own branded products. This should be your long term plan – you don't want to be a Shopify dropshipper forever – rather, you should be thinking of building your own brand.

29136388R00106

Printed in Great Britain
by Amazon